Getting Started in Unit and Investment Trusts

Acknowledgements

I am indebted to AA Arnaud's book 'Investment Trusts Explained'; David Cresswell for his work at the Investors Compensation Scheme compiling the 101 golden rules; Jonathan Fry of independent financial adviser Premier Investment Management; Michael Hughes, head of global economics and strategy, BZW, for information gleaned from his Gilt Equity Study; Neil McKendrick's pamphlet 'The Birth of Foreign & Colonial, The World's First Investment Trust'; Micropal, the firm of statisticians and in particular William White for his hard work; Peter Walls of securities house Credit Lyonnais Laing; Richard Wastcoat of Fidelity. Also Emma Weiss.

Both trade associations representing the investment fund industry (the Association of Investment Trust Companies and the Association of Unit Trust and Investment Funds) have given invaluable support.

I would also thank the countless others who have helped me gain sufficient knowledge and understanding of investment funds to be able to write this book.

Getting Started in Unit and Investment Trusts

Robert Cole

JOHN WILEY & SONS

Chichester • New York • Weinheim • Brisbane • Singapore • Toronto

Other Wiley Editorial Offices

John Wiley & Sons, Inc., 605 Third Avenue,
New York, NY 10158–0012, USA

Weinheim • Brisbane • Singapore • Toronto

Notice
Datastream is a registered trade name, trademark and service mark of Datastream International Limited.

All data and graphs contained in this publication and which have been obtained from the information system
of Datastream International Limited ("Datastream") are proprietary and confidential and may not be
reproduced, republished, redistributed or resold without the written permission of Datastream.

Data in Datastream's information system have been compiled by Datastream in good faith from sources
believed to be reliable, but no representation or warranty expressed or implied is made as to the accuracy,
completeness or correctness of the data. Neither Datastream nor such other party who may be the owner of any
information contained in the data accepts any liability whatsoever for any direct, indirect or consequential loss
arising from any use of the data or its contents. All data obtained from Datastream's system and contained in
this publication are for the assistance of users but are not to be relied upon as authoritative or taken in
substitution for the exercise of judgement or financial skills by users.

Library of Congress Cataloging-in-Publication Data

Cole, Robert, 1951–
    Getting started in unit and investment trusts / Robert Cole.
      p.   cm. — (Getting started in)
    Includes index.
    ISBN 0-471-96844-7 (pbk.)
    1. Mutual funds.   I. Title.   II.Series.
    HG4530.C565   1997
    332.63'27—dc21   96–39898
                                                  CIP

British Library Cataloguing in Publication Data

A catalogue record for this book is available from the British Library

ISBN 0-471-96844-7

wyn Ltd, Rowlands Castle, Hants
:d
ctured from sustainable forestation,
r paper production.

Contents

CHAPTER 1

An Introduction to Investment Funds: Share and Share Alike

This chapter introduces the basic mechanics and attraction of investment funds. It tells how investment funds can be the inflation-beating investment which spreads risk and provides exposure to markets where investors' expertise may not be great. It also explains how investment funds and personal equity plans (PEPs) fit together.

THE PROFIT PRINCIPLE

There is only one reason to save with an investment fund. To make money.

Investment funds are popular for the simple reason that they hold the potential for people to make more money than is possible with a bank or building society deposit account. That is a matter of historical fact (see Figure 1.1).

Saving with an investment fund is simply an easy means of investing in the stock market, and the stock market gives enhanced **returns**. Importantly, stock market investment also protects the value of money against the erosive effect of inflation.

return: another name for the profits on an investment. Losses are sometimes called negative returns.

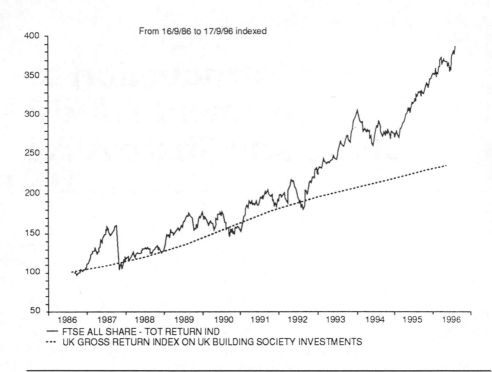

Figure 1.1   FTSE All Share against high interest building society deposit account. Source: Datastream. Reproduced by permission of Datastream International

unit trust: one of the two leading types of collective investment favoured by private investors. It is distinguished from an investment trust largely because the money it has to invest depends on investor demand. This is the so-called open ended structure.

Investment funds come in two types, **unit trusts** and **investment trusts**. There are clear technical differences in structure between unit and investment trusts but essentially both give easy access to assets normally traded by stock market professionals. As such unit and investment trusts are the ideal starting place for the novice stock market investor.

Equities are not the exclusive preserve of investment funds. Some invest in government loans, so called gilt-edged bonds. Corporate bonds and other money market instruments are also used. Some funds—property funds—invest directly into bricks and mortar. Some funds invest in bank deposits, and other hybrids appear from time to time with recent interest in funds investing in second-hand endowment policies. There are also a couple of Lloyd's of London investment trusts.

SAFE HAVENS

Investment funds collect different people's money. The money is pooled and used to buy a range of separate investments, most commonly shares. Investment funds are set up and administered by specialist fund management companies. But the funds and their assets are not owned by the fund management company. The owners are the individual savers.

The pool of investors employ a fund manager to manage the money, to invest it and get the best return possible. Individual investors select a fund manager from a wide range—most of whom are listed in Appendices 1 and 2 at the back of this book. Most commonly investors choose between funds that have been set up with particular aims. Investors have to examine the attractions and the drawbacks in each investment fund offering before coming to a decision.

After purchase, each individual saver owns a segment of the fund which is a miniature replica of the whole. If a fund owns 100 shares, each investor owns a part of each of those 100 shares. Investors therefore draw direct benefit if those shares rise in value, but also suffer if the shares disappoint.

With a unit trust assets are held in trust by independent trustees who also monitor the behaviour of the fund management company to ensure it is acting in the best interests of the investors. An investment trust company has a board of directors which performs a similar role.

Investment funds are designed with risk reduction in mind. The level of risk varies between funds, and can never be completely eliminated. However,

investment trust: one of the two leading types of investment fund favoured by private investors. It is distinguished from a unit trust largely because it has a fixed fund of money to use for investment. They are so-called closed end funds.

the collective nature of investment funds means they can confidently be thought of as a safe, or at least a safe-ish, haven.

BRINGING HOME THE BACON

The collective investment industry is hidebound with a lot of confusing and sometimes unnecessary detail and jargon. But for starters, just remember that when it comes to performance, shares and bonds generally outgun bank and building society deposits. Investment funds invest in shares and bonds.

If you invest for 10 years you can expect a building society to add perhaps 50–70% to the value of your money. With a stock market based investment such as a unit or investment trust you may reasonably hope that a lump sum of saving might triple in value. More importantly, the experience of the last 80 years or so strongly indicates that investing in equities means the real value of your money is maintained and enhanced. **Equities** are the inflation beater. If you rely on building societies and banks, on the other hand, the lesson of history is that the real value of your wealth can fall, eroded by inflation.

equity: another name for a share. Also sometimes called a security.

Unfortunately it is not all one way traffic with the stock market. In return for standing the chance to reap greater rewards, you also run greater risks. If you save with the building society there is virtually no chance you will lose your money and every chance that it will grow—albeit at a pedestrian pace. However, if you chase the bigger profit potential in the stock market you must be prepared to see the value of your savings fall.

Any investment decision boils down to balancing risk and reward. It is important to remember that there is a roughly proportional relationship between risk and reward. The more risk you are prepared to take that you will lose money, the more chance you will fill your boots. The less the risk you are prepared to countenance the less chance you will lose your shirt.

I have chosen two words in the last two paragraphs with particular care. The words are 'potential' and 'roughly'. With investment there is always room for doubt. For example, take almost any 5-year period in the last 50 and stock market investment will be shown to outstrip bank or building society deposits. But look hard enough and you will find an exception that proves the rule: for example, in the five year period between 1972 and 1977 you would have been better off in building society deposits than in equities.

SPREADING RISK

It would be wrong to wallow in the doubts and the downsides, however. Overwhelming evidence suggests that there is much more money to be made in the stock market than there is in banks or building societies. Moreover, one of the most popular attractions of collective investment is that the clear risk associated with stock market investment is reduced.

Risk is reduced because if one of the selected stocks bought by the fund fails the financial unpleasantness is spread among all the participating investors. Of course, rewards gained from the successes are diluted too: but reduced reward is the price paid for reduced risk. The total value of the unit or investment trust—and therefore the total value of each investor's savings—increases as long as the successes outweigh the failures.

As well as reducing risk, investment via collectives is easier. You could construct your own private, diversified, portfolio of shares but this involves making perhaps 15 or 20 purchases. That involves at least as many different investment decisions and means you incur multiple sets of transaction charges.

In practice this is feasible only for quite well-off investors—those who have a minimum £20,000 earmarked for the stock market. Doing it yourself also means that you must possess the correct mix of expertise, luck and courage to make a series of individual investment decisions. It also presumes you have the time and inclination to monitor, assess and make changes to the portfolio.

By using an investment fund the process is simplified. You still need expertise, luck and courage—but not in such vast quantities. It also makes stock market investment accessible to less well-off people—with as little as £250 to start off with, or £25 a month in a regular savings scheme.

You can buy into a collective investment vehicle by writing one cheque. The creation of a well-spread personal portfolio means writing dozens.

In the same way tax computations are much simplified. Allying a collective investment with the tax-free status of a PEP negates any need for tax calculations altogether.

Collectives give small investors access to economies of scale normally reserved for their much larger brethren. Do it yourself and as a small operator you will be subject to the most expensive tariff regimes for buying and selling shares. Link with others and the collective weight of money will talk the price of dealing down.

EXPOSE YOURSELF

There is a further reason to invest in funds rather than directly into shares which is that for a British person it is extremely difficult to do anything but trade British company shares. There are a handful of US and European stocks quoted on the London Stock Exchange but to buy shares in foreign companies really means dealing with overseas exchanges.

That is difficult enough in itself, but one or a combination of the following factors could turn difficult into impossible: time zone differences, language, settlement of bills, transfer of money, custody of shares, local regulatory frameworks, taxation. And how do you conduct research on foreign companies to know which ones to invest in?

Many professional investors and large institutions focus on UK company shares, and it is a respectable—if limiting—policy to adopt. However, skilful use of investment funds means it becomes practically possible for British investors to expose themselves to overseas equity markets. Aggressive investors wanting capital growth from firms based in emerging economies, as well as cautious investors who want exposure to the broadest geographical spread, will require this facility.

FOR BIG FISH AND SMALL FRY

Collectives are particularly handy for people who have relatively small savings. But they are also used by bigger investors. Rich individuals and multi-million pound investment institutions use collectives in conjunction with direct share purchases for what is essentially the same reason that small, inexperienced investors use them: they want to spread risk and take advantage of someone else's investment management expertise.

At the same time, investors large and small can use an investment in a collective as a way of acquiring knowledge. You can obtain valuable experience and expertise of a particular stock market through a collective before moving on to invest directly in individual company shares.

But where the small savers may use a collective to gain entry to the most famous stock markets, the larger player will use collectives for more particular purposes—for example to invest in stock markets of South East Asia or in companies that specialise in oil and gas exploration. Big investors are confident enough to trust their own judgement for stocks and shares they know about but are perfectly happy to take expert advice where their knowledge is thin.

So take a leaf out of the professional's book. When putting an exploratory foot in a stock market pond, cover it with a collective investment fund wellington boot.

PEPS

Many private investors are attracted by PEPs and perhaps believe them to be an investment vehicle in themselves. But this is not strictly true. A PEP gives an investment tax exemption, rather than being an investment in its own right. A PEP should be thought of as nothing more than a tax shelter. A PEP does not bring profits in itself, but merely protects investment profits from tax.

PEPs and investment are best thought of separately but the two fit together as a partnership in which investment returns can be enhanced by freeing investment profits from tax liabilities. PEPs should by no means be ignored, but the PEP should not be the focus of attention. The underlying investment is much more important because profits come from the investment, not the tax-sheltering structure that can be erected around it.

Investment funds are well suited to playing the lead role in this partnership. It is also very popular to use investment funds in PEPs with two out of three PEPs being dedicated to investment fund investment. As a result, this book is designed to be a companion for the 'PEP investor' every bit as much as it is designed to help those interested in finding out about investment funds.

CHAPTER 2

Collectives in Context: The History and Growth of Unit and Investment Trusts

This chapter will overview the rising popularity of unit and investment trusts in Britain during the past 130 years. Comparison will be made with similar vehicles in Europe, North America, the Far East and elsewhere.

THE OLD ONES ARE THE BEST

The oldest ideas are invariably the best and investment funds are as old as the hills. From the beginning of time—or at least since folk have exchanged goods and service in trade—people have been clubbing together to make their wealth work in the most effective way. Investment funds have not always been in the form of the highly regulated, specialised, hyper-analysed financial instruments we have today. But when the first ancient Egyptian shook hands on an ox-sharing deal with his next-door neighbour the investment fund was born.

Investment funds are about three things: reducing costs, reducing risk and sharing profits. Messrs Nepthiti and Zofrah did precisely this with their ox: by buying the animal its cost was split. They spread both the initial purchase price and the annual management cost of feed and shelter. Risk was also halved because there were two of them to guard against theft. If the animal became lame, or died, the loss carried by each man was also less, reduced to the cost of half an ox. But the benefits were shared. Neither man needed the full services of a whole ox, and a time-sharing arrangement meant the ox's strength was put to the best use.

The greatest English playwright also had a good grasp of the benefits of collective investment. In his play the *Merchant of Venice* sixteenth-century William Shakespeare had Antonio—the selfsame merchant—say to his friends Salanio and Salarino:

> My ventures are not in one bottom trusted,
> Nor to one place; nor is my whole estate
> Upon the fortune of this present year;
> Therefore my merchandise makes me not sad.

This short extract from a play written in 1598 primarily deals with risk reduction, but if one assumes Antonio cooperated with others in order to be able to afford stakes in several different 'bottoms' (boats), reward sharing and cost efficiency follow shortly from the subtext. Best of all, however, Antonio displays his peace of mind at having—effectively—entered into an investment fund arrangement.

Peace of mind is something that is never comprehensive when it comes to investment, but if you select a good fund manager and approach with the right attitude you can use investment funds with a high level of assurance. Individual investors themselves have overall responsibility, but by buying into investment funds the details can be left to others, while you work, or play, in other areas.

THE BIRTH OF MODERN INVESTMENT FUNDS—1868

Despite the longevity of the idea of pooled investment it is still a surprise to most people that the first investment fund—in format immediately recognisable by the modern day investor—was launched as early as 1868. The first investment fund was an investment trust, and it is still in existence today. The Foreign & Colonial Investment Trust (F&CIT) is not only one of the oldest established funds, it is also among the most successful. There are 17 investment trusts in the international general category defined by the Association of Investment Trust Companies and used by Micropal statisticians and over 10 years F&CIT comes in the top five. If you had given £1000 to F&CIT 10 years ago your fund would be worth £4000. This is not the best, but it is quite comfortably ahead of the average.

It is a surprise to some people that the first investment fund took the form of an investment trust, a vehicle constituted under company law. Unit trusts, largely thanks to less strict advertising restraints, are more widely known about and commonly thought to predate investment trusts. They do not. Unit trusts came on the scene relatively late, in the 1930s. It is also enough to raise an eyebrow to learn that the F&CIT, and indeed most trusts launched before the First World War, had little or nothing to do with shares. Today investment funds are thought of as vehicles to get exposure to equities. However, the first trusts invested in government loans. In the mid nineteenth century shares were not common. Companies—like the emerging railway operators and mill owners— raised money by borrowing money from investors. Governments also borrowed.

British government loans became known as gilts because the paper loan agreements issued to investors were bordered with gold leaf, a sign of creditworthiness—that investors would get their money back on the pre-agreed date and that they would receive interest payments on time. It was largely because of the enormous resources and technological skills available from the Empire that British government debt was the most reliable. But by being reliable the British government could also afford to pay mean rates of interest. A typical return would have been 3% a year.

Pioneers like Lord Westbury (Figure 2.1), who was the first chairman of the F&CIT, noticed that overseas governments paid better returns. Rates of up to 8% a year were available. But the risks were also higher. The solution, and the way to gain access to the high returns, was to invest money in a range of high-paying stocks. Some might slip through by failing, but if the net spread was wide enough and the defaults few enough the overall fund would not be knocked too far off a profitable course.

Buying into a portfolio meant risk was spread, not eliminated. Risk is never completely eliminated. None the less the first investors had a crucial judgement to make, and one which lies at the heart of investment fund decisions today. It was to assess whether the greater potential rewards available from the foreign country loans were worth the larger risk that the investments may fail. The benchmark was the British government stock, now called the gilt. They could get 3% a year at minimal risk, so what extra reward was necessary to make it worth while running the additional risk?

The fact that the F&C fund worked, was replicated, and is still in existence is perhaps the best evidence that the first investors got the judgement broadly right. It has never been one-way traffic, but

Figure 2.1   Lord Westbury, first chairman of Foreign & Colonial, the first investment trust

millions of investors over the generations provide a wealth of evidence that the formula does work.

The first investment fund portfolio put together by the F&C pioneers consisted of 18 different stocks, or loans, issued by countries as diverse as Argentina and Turkey and from as far apart as Nova Scotia and New South Wales. Investments were made in countries like the United States of America which have flourished and in 'Danubian' loans originating from a nation which no longer exists and of which I have never heard. In point of fact not all 18 of the loan stocks were issued by governments. One was the Egyptian Railway Loan, a stock issued by a more entrepreneurial and specific minded enterprise. It was not long into the history of investment funds that foreign government bonds were joined in much greater strength by loans to private companies.

A copy of one of the first investment trust portfolio schedules is reproduced in Figure 2.2.

THE IDEA CATCHES ON

In 1870 a 25-year-old clerk from Dundee went to America at the behest of his mill-owning boss. When Robert Fleming returned in 1873, he had told his friends and business associates of the tremendous investment opportunities in the New World. He, too, set up an investment trust and called it the Scottish American Investment Trust. It was the first of many to emanate from an investment management operation that still thrives today, and which proudly bears the Robert Fleming name. Save & Prosper, one of the larger unit trust management groups which is perhaps better known for sponsoring international rugby union fixtures at Twickenham, is part of the same group.

In 1875, eight years after the birth of the F&CIT, there were 18 others up and running. Investments

THE

FOREIGN AND COLONIAL GOVERNMENT TRUST COMPANY, LIMITED.

A Complete List of the Securities held by the Company on January 10th, 1885.

NOMINAL AMOUNT.	NAME OF SECURITY.
£	
93,080	Alabama Coal, Iron, Land and Colonization Co., Limited Instalment Certificates (*Formerly £71,600 Alabama 8 p.ct. State Bonds.*)
1,074	Ditto ditto ditto B Shares
4,160	Alabama 6 per cent. State Bonds (Class A).
14,700	Alagoas Railway Company, Limited, 6 per cent. Debentures.
*9,600	Amoor River Navigation Company, 2 per cent.
28,600	Argentine 6 per cent., 1871 (Public Works).
69,518 15s.	Ditto ditto 1872 (Hard Dollars).
9,600	Ditto ditto 1882.
9,000	Austrian 4 per cent. Gold Rentes.
229,815	Ditto 5 per cent., 1868 (Silver Loan).
25,000	Barbados Railway Company, Limited, 5½ per cent. Mortgage Debentures
10,000	Brazil, Great Western of, Railway Company, Limited, 7 per cent. Shares.
17,200	Brazilian 5 per cent., 1865.
10,000	Ditto ditto 1875.
22,500	Ditto 4½ per cent., 1879. (Internal Loan).
5,000	Ditto 4½ per cent., 1883.
27,100	Brazilian Imperial Central Bahia Railway Company, Limited, 6 per cent. Debentures.
30,000	Ditto ditto ditto 6 per cent. Debenture Stock.
24,920 (1,246 Shares.)	Ditto ditto ditto 7 per cent. Shares.
3,500	Buenos Ayres, 6 per cent., 1824.
10,000	Ditto 6 per cent., 1882.
29,000	Buenos Ayres Western Railway of, 6 per cent. Debentures.
10,000	Buenos Ayres and Pacific Railway Company, Limited, 7 per cent. Debenture Stock.
30,000 (1,500 Shares.)	Canadian Pacific Railway Company. Capital Stock.
3,000	Cape of Good Hope Government, 4½ per cent. Loan.
10,000	Central Argentine Railway Company Stock.
27,000	Chilian 4½ per cent., 1858.
21,000	Ditto 7 per cent., 1866.
28,800	Ditto 6 per cent., 1867.
9,000	Ditto 5 per cent., 1870.
17,000	Ditto 5 per cent., 1873.
19,500	Ditto 5 per cent., 1875.
7,500	City of Auckland 5 per cent., Debentures, 1883.
5,000	City of Christchurch (N.Z.) 6 per cent.
7,000	City of Melbourne (Victoria) 4½ per cent, 1883.
10,100	City of Mobile (Alabama) 3 per cent. to 5 per cent.
1,500	City of Montreal (Canada) 5 per cent. Debentures.
5,000	City of Wellington (N.Z.) 6 per cent. Waterworks Loan.
10,000	Cobourg Harbour (Canada) 6 per cent.
*12,600	Colombian 4¾ per cent. State Bonds, 1873.
8,700	Danubian 7 per cent., 1864.
14,950	Ditto 8 per cent., 1867.
19,800	Donna Thereza Christina Railway Company, Limited, 5½ per cent. Debentures.
16,000 (1,000 Shares.)	Dunaburg and Witepsk Railway Company, Limited, 5 per cent. Shares.
143,680	Egyptian 5 per cent. Preference Stock.
93,300	Ditto 5 per cent. State Domain.
85,133. 6/8	French 3 per cent. Rentes.
30,000	Georgia 7 per cent. Gold Bonds.
690	Hamburg City Lottery 3 per cent.
23,592	Hungarian 5 per cent., 1867, Railways.

NOMINAL AMOUNT.	NAME OF SECURITY.
£	
17,500	Hungarian 5 per cent., 1871, State Loan.
19,900	Ditto 5 per cent., 1873, ditto.
66,750	Ditto 6 per cent., 1875, Gold Loan.
10,000 (700,000 Rs.)	India Government 4 per cent. Enfaced Paper.
64,000	Ditto 4½ per cent. Rupee Paper.
6,000	Ditto ditto Inscribed at the Bank of England.
900	Italian 6 per cent. Irrigation.
107,280	Ditto 5 per cent. Maremmana Railway.
176,660	Ditto 5 per cent. Rentes.
12,900	Japan 7 per cent., 1873.
5,940	Kaschau Oderberger Railway 5 per cent.
32,940	Lemberg, Czernowitz, & Jassy Railway 7 per cent. Shares.
19,140	Lombardo-Venetian Railway 3 per cent. Obligations.
592. 10/.	Lubeck City 3½ per cent. Lottery Loan.
5,000	Lyttelton Harbour Board (N.Z.) 6 per cent.
7,200	Missouri 6 per cent. State Bonds.
23,000	New Zealand Government 5 per cent. Consolidated Bonds.
7,000	New Zealand Government 4 per cent. Inscribed Stock.
10,000	Oamaru Harbour (N.Z.) 6 per cent., 1879.
5,490	Oldenburg Lottery 3 per cent.
140,000	Portuguese 3 per cent., 1880.
10,800	Queensland Government 4 per cent. Debentures.
17,400	Recife Drainage Company (Brazil) 5 per cent.
55,000 (2,200 Shares.)	Rio de Janeiro City Improvements Company Shares.
66,520	Roumanian 6 per cent. State Obligations.
10,100	Ditto 5 per cent. Redeemable Rentes.
8,000	Ditto 5 per cent., 1875 (Public Debt).
34,154. 5/.	Russian Anglo-Dutch 5 per cent., 1866.
199,820	Ditto 4 per cent. Nicolai Railway.
19,500	Santa Fé 6 per cent., 1883.
6,300	Servian 5 per cent. Redeemable Rentes.
116,000	South Austrian Lombardo-Venetian 3 per cent. Obligations. Series X.
177,020	South Italian Railways 3 per cent. Obligations.
15,500 (775 Shares.)	Southern Brazilian Rio Grande Do Sul Railway Shares.
28,260	Ditto ditto 6 per cent. Debenture Stock
2,500 (500 Shares.)	Southern Mahratta Railway Company, Limited, Shares.
200,617. 17/4	Spanish Government 4 per cent.
29,877. 10/.	Ditto 2 per cent.
7,120	Stuhl-Weissenburg-Raab-Grazer 4 per cent. Mortgage Bonds.
4,350	Ditto ditto 4 per cent. Lottery Loan.
136,900	Turkish 5 per cent., 1854 (Tribute Loan).
33,500	Ditto 6 per cent., 1858 (Registered).
16,300	Ditto 6 per cent., 1862 (Registered).
100,000	Ditto 4¼ per cent., 1871 (Tribute Loan).
10,000	Ditto 5 per cent., 1877, Ottoman Defence Loan.
*9,600	Ditto 6 per cent. Roumelian Railways.
8,000	Uruguay 5 per cent., 1883.
5,000	Valparaiso Drainage Company, Limited, 6 per cent. Mortgage Debentures.
*20,000	Varna Railway Company 3 per cent. Obligations.
*5,000	Ditto 3 per cent. Shares.
59,680	Victor Emmanuel Railway Company 3 per cent. Obligations.
*10,600 ($53,000.)	Virginia 10/40 Bonds.
*46.000 ($230,000.)	Ditto 6 per cent. New Funded.
20,000	Western Australia Public Works 5 per cent.

Figure 2.2 Schedule of F&C first portfolio

were made in the British railway companies, mining outfits, telegraph operators, shipping and manufacturing. In those early days, however, investments meant lending money and the aim was to earn income. The early trusts were keen to get their

dividend: the annual, twice yearly, quarterly or monthly payments made to shareholders as an income on shares they own.

original investment back at the end of a loan agreement, but did not expect to see capital rise in value. In fact it was not until after the First World War that shares—where capital growth is the name of the game, and income through **dividends** is a side order—became widely available and were included in investment fund portfolios.

Equities grew in popularity because inflation spread its wings. Inflation erodes the buying power of money and when inflation runs loose it is not enough to get the same amount of capital back at the end of a funding period as you supplied at the start. In real terms, £100 in 1950 was only worth £67 in 1960, for instance. Some compensation could be given from higher interest rates on fixed capital return loan stocks, but shares—where the capital value could grow with inflation—offered a much better bet for savers who were worried about rising prices and the eroding effect on the value of money.

It is also interesting to note—considering how the original investment funds worked—that in the UK collective investment vehicles all but forgot about bonds in the 1980s and early 1990s. But—albeit helped by a favourable tax change—the mid 1990s have seen a rebirth in the popularity of bonds among private investors. It is probably not a coincidence that this resurging preference for bonds has come at a time when inflation rates have been subdued.

FOSTER AND THE FIRST FRAUD

Two other lessons can be drawn from the history books. One is that it did not take long for the first fraud to be perpetrated. In 1879 a clerk by the name of Clement J. Foster was found with his hands in the till. He stole eight bonds and £5 10 shillings, and was sent to prison with hard labour for 12 months. Even by the standards of the time it was a fairly minor offence, and the stiff reaction also owes much to the sterner Victorian attitudes to crime and punishment. However, it also demonstrates that the administrators of investment funds have always been, and continue to be, petrified by embezzlement, fraud and any wrongdoing that could undermine confidence by the individual investors.

The history of the investment fund movement is littered with Clement J. Fosters. Many—including the 1990s bogeyman Robert Maxwell—were far more sinister. But for the continuing and sustainable health of the investment fund movement it is most important that the clients have trust. Reputable operators know they will earn far more money through legal appropriation from satisfied customers of small percentage management fees over many years than they will by engaging in acts of plunder.

THE INEVITABLE INVESTMENT FUND ROLLER COASTER

The second lesson from the archives is that investment funds have ridden a roller coaster of boom and bust ever since they appeared on the scene. In the 1870s some funds suffered as a recession prompted more lenders to default than was expected. By 1888 to 1889 it was back to excitement only for the first Barings crisis to bring investors back to earth again.

The Barings crisis of 1890 was precipitated when a period of overenthusiasm about investment prospects in Latin America came to an end. Authorities could not blame a 'rogue' Singapore-based derivatives trader, as happened in 1995, but both knocks share the same essence. In both cases disaster struck because wishful thinking was allowed to replace sound, cool-headed, investment analysis.

Calm returned and the investment fund movement steadily grew up to 1914. War brought upheaval, and in the aftermath depressed commodity prices did more damage to funds. Recovery followed and in the pre-1929 bull run investment funds prospered. But the depression of the 1930s and war in the 1940s caused the longest and most pronounced slump in the movement's 130-year history.

During the 1950s and 1960s investment funds recouped, only to run into the 1973 oil crisis. Then there was Margaret Thatcher's popular capitalism which ran to a peak in October 1987.

Greed, and perhaps fear, are the primary reasons why investment fund history tracks this boom–bust roller coaster. Ignorance plays an important part too. Investors get carried away and as long as prices are rising few people are concerned enough to find out whether the increases are sustainable.

Stock market investment has a great deal in common with horse-race gambling. Both are about staking money in the hope of making more money. Both are also about making choices about how exactly to go about fulfilling this aim. But, in the sensible world at least, the two activities should be kept at different ends of the spectrum. Investment is a serious activity, horse-race gambling is leisure. It is usually the case that when investment creeps too far along the spectrum towards gambling things go wrong.

Astute investors will recognise what represents sustainable growth and what is irresponsible silliness. However, very astute investors will also give themselves measured exposure to unrealistically enthusiastic bull runs. After all, if prices are going up there is little point in turning away just because you believe the rises to be unsustainable. Few people got far in investment by rigidly sticking to principles.

If you are to take advantage of other investors' herd tendencies you have to be very nimble. You must sell and buy back investments at frequent intervals in order to lock in profits. You must also gradually reduce your total holdings in the volatile investments as the prices rise. Having said that you do not need to be that kind of astute investor to profit from stock markets. One of the main attractions of investment funds such as unit and investment trusts is that you employ someone else to do the expert foot shuffling.

Perhaps more importantly stock market investment should be viewed as a long-term activity. Dipping in and out of markets for short-term profit can work but the real beauty of investment funds for private individuals is that they produce good returns over long periods—and long means at least five years, preferably ten years or more.

Peaks are followed by troughs which are followed by peaks and more troughs. That is the pattern from the past and there is no reason to assume things will change. It is important to appreciate, however, that the bottom of each successive trough has been higher than the previous one. This evidence should be enough to give long-term investors the confidence to accept the risks.

THE OVERSEAS EXPERIENCE

Investment funds were born and bred in Britain but it was not long before North America took up the idea and it is probably fair to say that the true home of investment funds is now on the other side of the Atlantic.

Pure size is the first reason why North America is the home of the investment fund. In the USA investment funds are called mutual funds and their total value dwarfs the size of what the rest of the world supports. Figures collected at the end of February 1996 showed there was more than US$3000 billion (aboout £2000 billion) invested in US-based mutual funds. That is about three-fifths of the total amount invested all across the globe.

The second reason why I call the USA the home of the mutual fund is perhaps more telling. The investment funds movement finds its home in North America because that is the home of the consumer investment market. A conservative estimate is that 40 million Americans own mutual investment funds. If two Americans meet outside their homeland the first question they want to know the answer to is where the other person is from. But after 'So where you from?' comes 'D'ya know what the Dow's at?'

Ordinary people invest as a part of everyday existence. Many buy and sell individual stocks but the mutual fund industry is also more advanced and better utilised. The level of investment expertise among Americans is many times more advanced than in Britain and there is a tendency, which I regard as positive, for individuals to accept and look for much more responsibility in the arrangement of their financial security and the health of their long-term wealth.

In the USA and in other foreign countries mutual funds are structured more like our unit trusts than the older established investment trusts. Worldwide, it is more usual to see so-called open-ended investment funds rather than closed-end vehicles. In Japan investment funds go by two names. Both varieties, as in the USA, are organised in open-ended structures, but slightly different funds are used by corporations who have spare money to invest and want to put it into pooled equity funds. These, and I am using a phonetic spelling here, are called *tokkin*. Funds for individuals owe part of their name to the English-speaking world. They go by the name *open toshi shintaku* and again I use a phonetic spelling. Total fund value in Japan is about US$500 billion (£330 billion).

In Continental Europe the French market, with *sicavs*, is the largest although Luxembourg-based funds are also significant, particularly as a home for equity investors in Germany.

Many French funds are equity oriented but the French market has grown larger because of demand for money market funds. These funds, available in Britain and elsewhere and which are sometimes called cash funds, invest in bank deposits. But because they are well resourced and can deposit large sums of cash the money market funds are able to demand the very best rates of interest. Smaller investors, with smaller sums to deposit, invariably have to make do with inferior rates.

In Britain money market funds are not popular because it is perceived that the fees attached to investment fund structures quickly erode the benefits of better interest rates that pooling brings. However, many of these funds carry lighter charges than equivalent equity or bond funds. Smaller investors can tap into respectable, if not market beating rates by using these funds.

For historical reasons connected with official regulation the French banking system has not provided small savers with rates which even approach the best available to the big depositors. The attraction of pooling savings into a money market *sicav*, therefore, is greater. Yes, there are *sicav* fees but the greater disparity between interest rates available to large and small investors makes these charges worth paying.

I have surveyed the leading countries where collective investment vehicles are used. But they exist in other places, in fact in any place where the financial infrastructure is solid enough to support the confidence of the private investor. The birth and growth of a collective investment industry—as are currently being witnessed in India and South East Asian countries—are perhaps a good sign of genuine economic progress.

3 CHAPTER

Unit Trusts and Investment Trusts: They Are the Same, Only Different

U nit trusts and investment trusts are in many ways very much alike but there are important technical differences. This chapter explains the similarities and the differences. It will stress that investment trusts have the capacity to fulfil more specialist functions using split capital structures. Investment trusts also have the capacity to borrow money and, arguably, managers have more freedom to make share and stock dealing decisions.

WHAT IS IN A NAME?

collective investment: another name for a unit trust or an investment trust. Also called pooled investments, mutual funds and investment funds.

Unit trusts and investment trusts are badly named. For one thing an investment trust is not even a trust, it is a company. A name should explain what a particular thing is. Neither 'unit trust' nor 'investment trust' conforms to this blindingly obvious piece of common sense.

Unit and investment trusts are sometimes called **collective investment** schemes. Another name for them is pooled investment vehicles. These are better because they acknowledge a central strength of unit and investment trusts which is that there is safety in numbers.

But unit and investment trusts are best called mutual investment funds. That is what they are known as in the United States, and it is a name which explains and defines what unit and investment trusts are.

The term 'mutual' indicates that the funds are run for the shared benefit of investors. 'Investment' is a term broad enough to encapsulate the diverse objectives of different funds, but is also narrow enough to make it clear they are about making money for investors. 'Fund' is a useful suffix because it hints at the in-built investment strength.

In this book I shall refer to unit trusts and investment trusts as investment funds. It is the commonly used British term which corresponds closest to the US name.

TAX

Investment funds have an advantage over individuals, and ordinary trading companies, when it comes to investment. Neither a unit trust nor an investment trust pays tax on its investments. Profits from investments are therefore enhanced. Tax is paid by investors—unless other exemptions are used—but it is incurred outside the funds, not internally.

STUFF AND NONSENSE

It is important not to be befuddled by the twin-track approach which exists within the UK investment fund industry in Britain. The novice consumer should understand that there is much more holding unit trusts and investment trusts together than there is separating them.

The two types of investment fund share basic principles and aims. In the beginning the novice investor could easily think of the two as being identical. Perhaps too often the first question posed by those approaching investment in collective vehicles is 'Ought I go for a unit trust or an investment trust?' when in fact there are much more important decisions to be made. Like: 'What kind of risk am I prepared to take on?' 'Do I want to be in equities or bonds?' 'Do I have a lump sum to invest or am I thinking of saving smaller amounts regularly?' 'Have I studied comparative investment performance statistics?' 'Do I understand that equity investment requires patience?' 'What are the charges?' 'Is it worth while wrapping my investment fund into a PEP?'

It is questions such as these which are important. In answering them and finding an investment fund which provides the right solutions you will probably come across both unit trusts and investment trusts. But your specific choice of fund depends on factors far more important than whether a fund goes under the unit trust or the investment trust code.

Remember the bare essential: both pool the savings of many people to spread risk and enhance returns.

Promoters of unit trusts and promoters of investment trusts spend far too much time, money and energy trying to mark out differences between the two genres and far too little time, money and energy establishing the common ground. Investment trusts have their trade association, called the Association of Investment Trust Companies, the AITC. The unit trust industry has an equivalent, called the Association of Unit Trusts and Investment Funds—or AUTIF for short. Both bodies make continuous strenuous efforts to, quite rightly, point out that pooled investment is one of the best ways for novice investors to gain access to the stock market. Both associations never stop telling anybody willing to listen that collective investment is the easiest and cheapest way into equities and bonds. Individual companies and fund management groups—on whose behalf the trade associations act—do the same. But while there is absolutely nothing wrong with the message, or indeed with either the unit trust or investment trust format, the message is muddied. Intentionally and unintentionally, the two rival industry trade associations snipe at each other. The effect is to shoot one another in the foot.

To an outside commentator this situation is made even more bizarre because several high profile fund management companies—including Fidelity, Kleinwort Benson, Henderson Touche Remnant, GT and M&G—operate under both codes. History and pride, no doubt, stand in the way of sensible *rapprochement* but if peace were to break out, both sides would benefit from the increased clarity of purpose to achieve increased sales, and profits.

This annoying marketing spat is of no direct relevance to the private investor. But indirectly it has quite substantial implications. It puts private investors off investing in the stock market, and therefore it closes lucrative avenues of opportunity to thousands, probably millions, of people.

One day the vested interests that make up the membership of AUTIF and the AITC might see sense. But in the mean time it is vital that private investors should not be put off by this ridiculous behaviour. Collective investment—be it through a unit trust, an investment trust or through one of the newfangled open-ended investment companies —is, on the whole, a good thing. The rest is secondary.

VARIETY AND SPICE

The differences between unit and investment trusts are of secondary importance, but they are not irrelevant. To say it is silly that the two codes belittle each other is not to say that the two sides should merge into an indistinguishable whole. Quite the reverse. The differences should be preserved. The differences expand the usefulness of the investment fund movement, and broaden the opportunities for enrichment.

So what is the difference between a unit trust and an investment trust? Essentially it lies in the distinctive internal structures upon which the two varieties of collective investment fund are hung.

A COMPANY NOT A TRUST

An investment trust is not a trust at all. It is only an accident of history that they are called trusts, and it is off-putting. Investment trusts are companies, whose business—instead of manufacturing, say, lollipops—is to buy and sell shares and other investment assets.

An investment trust company's business is fund management. Like all companies its *raison d'être* is to make its shareholders richer, but where a conventional company might do this by making lollipops, an investment trust company aims to enrich its owners by buying and selling shares and other investment assets.

An investment trust company has the same obligations as any other Stock Exchange listed company. It has a board of directors, it has an obligation to report financial results and it has shareholders. The shareholders are the investors in the investment trust company. So where a unit trust has unit holders, an investment trust has shareholders.

WHERE WILL IT ALL END?

To lapse into jargon for a moment, unit trusts are *open-ended* and investment trusts are *closed-ended*. In translation, the open-ended structure of a unit trust means that its size is unrestricted. It does not matter how many investors want to take part, nor how much money is pooled, because in a unit trust the amount of money that can be collected together for investment is limitless. Shares, bonds and other assets are simply bought and sold by the fund managers to reflect the amount of money being saved in the unit trust by investors.

The size of an investment trust, however, is limited. A fixed amount of money is raised during a launch period, and that same pot of money is invested and reinvested during the investment trust's life. The value of the original money invested will change—hopefully grow—whether we are talking about a unit or an investment trust. But with an investment trust the original amount of money raised, the so-called issued share capital, stays the same.

This is a simplification. Investment trust companies can raise new money by holding a rights issue, a money-raising mechanism which is used by all Stock Exchange quoted companies. Many reputable investment trust companies do not like holding rights issues, however, because the process can dilute value in the trust, particularly if existing shareholders do not want to take up their rights to new shares issued. Investment trust company fund managers may bleat that they need more money to take advantage of exciting new opportunities but purists will counter that the fund manager should be making money on other investments, or be shuffling the portfolio in order to take advantage of opportunities without needing any new money. An investment trust manager will want to raise more money, however, because if there is more money being managed the income from the annual management charge paid by investors is enhanced.

The lesson for investors is to avoid an investment trust company which seems to have lots of rights issues. Growth by additional subscription is illusory growth, just like it is when a trading company tries to grow by acquiring other companies. The sustainable indicator of success is genuine underlying asset value development, measurable on a like-for-like basis.

Because it is both unwise and unfashionable for investment trust companies to have rights issues, other devices have been dreamed up which allow investment trust companies to raise new money, as it were on the sly.

It is perhaps a bit unfair to say the mechanisms are sly because they can hold advantages for shareholders. But it is as well to be aware of the cynics' view, even if it is only to be able to watch out for abuses. The first method is to issue warrants to shareholders. The owner of a **warrant** has the right to buy a new share in a particular company at a pre-agreed price at a pre-specified date in the future. If the pre-agreed price is attractive when the right-to-buy date comes round, the warrant holder will buy. But in doing so he or she gives new money to the investment company which increases the number of shares in issue and which can dilute value in the same way a rights issue would do.

warrant: an option to buy or not to buy investment trust shares at a specified future date.

The warrant owner does not have to buy, he or she just has the right to buy. If the price at which the warrant can be exercised is less than the market price of the shares, it will be worth buying. But the market price may be below, making it unprofitable to exercise the right to buy warrants.

Again, because an investment trust company is a company, it is bound by the same rules as any other: any company can issue warrants attached to shares, but it is a practice used by investment trust companies more than others. Warrants are often issued at launch, at the same time ordinary shares are issued.

It might be useful to note at this point that warrants can be traded separately from ordinary shares between the issue date and the time of exercise. The investment management skills to do this, however, are advanced largely because elements of doubt, and therefore risk, are greater than for managing ordinary shares—be they in investment trust companies or trading companies. Investment funds, both unit and investment trusts, exist which specialise in warrants.

One of the main uses of warrants is to add incentive and encourage loyalty in much the same way that share options are issued to directors and workers in ordinary trading companies. But in a new investment company launch the attachment of warrants can also have the effect of phasing the money-raising period. It is quite often wise to drip-feed cash into any sort of investment and warrants help the achievement of this objective.

Another device used to meet this drip-feed ambition is to issue so-called 'C' shares. But where warrants delay the time when investors actually stump up the cash, 'C' shares are paid for in full at the outset, but run in parallel to the main shares until a pre-agreed time when they convert into ordinary shares.

'C' shares get their name because some companies, not just investment trust companies, issue shares which have different rights attached to them. Commonly it was 'A' and 'B' shares, and the difference was in the voting rights attached. Family-owned firms where founders wanted to keep control of the business were prone to issue shares which carried variable amounts of influence. In essence, the 'A', 'B' or 'C' classification just means the shares are the same in some ways, but different in others.

SPLIT PERSONALITIES

As I have said earlier, it is vital to understand that unit trusts and investment trusts are very much alike. For the novice investor the common ground is also much more important than the technical differences that separate the two varieties of investment fund.

Unit trust structures are simpler, which in some circumstances is a plus point. But investment trusts, in being able to adopt more complex structures, have advantages in flexibility.

One such complication is to be able to split a single share into constituent parts, as is done by split capital investment trusts. Most forms of investment, and equity investment is a classic example, produces profit in two ways, firstly in value growth and secondly in income via dividends. An investment in pharmaceuticals giant Glaxo Wellcome, for example, returns profits via an increasing share price, and in dividends.

Many investors are happy to receive both kinds of profit. Some, however, perhaps for tax reasons, will prefer either capital growth or income growth. As is explained in Chapter 5, unit and investment trusts exist which have the aim of identifying investments where one or other of these two profit types is predominant.

Split capital investment trusts go one step further. The underlying investment is made in standard capital and income-producing assets, but the benefits accruing from each kind of profit are attributed to different classes of shareholder. The profits stream is split by the trust managers so that capital shareholders get all the capital growth, and the income shareholders get all the dividends.

The effect is to increase the capital profit payable to capital shareholders and to increase the income for income shareholders. But only, of course, because the capital–income counterparts surrender the element they do not want.

Two other similar hybrids are 'zero dividend preference shares' and 'stepped preference shares'. 'Zeros', as the name implies, give capital growth with no dividends while stepped preference shares are income producers, and the amount of income steps steadily upwards during the life of the investment.

All split capital investment trusts have a fixed life span. On the winding-up date usually 10 years or so from launch the assets are liquidated and handed back to shareholders in accordance with their entitlement.

The term 'preference' relates to the class of share, and compares with the term 'ordinary' shares which is what most investment trust and other company shares are called. Preference shareholders hold a slightly more secure form of investment than ordinary shareholders because preference shareholders get preference in the credit queue should a company be wound up. But in exchange for this security the returns are usually less good.

One other type of investment trust share is called 'highly geared ordinary shares'. These sit at the other end of the spectrum from preference shares and come last in the creditors' winding-up queue, after normal ordinary shares. But greater risk of loss is rewarded with greater potential profit. The balancing act between risk and reward is a recurrent theme in all aspects of investment.

AN OPEN AND CLOSED CASE

The differences between a unit trust and an investment trust spark a thousand arguments among investment fund aficionados. The unit trust fan will say that the open-ended structure is best because it means the unit price always directly reflects the value of the underlying assets.

Investment trusts are often dogged by the seemingly illogical problem that the price of the investment trust share does not mirror the value of the underlying assets. It is quite usual for an investment trust share to trade at, say, 80p when the value of the underlying asset is, say, 90p. In such a case the investment trust shares are said to trade at a discount to net asset value (NAV). The breadth of discount to NAV varies from time to time, and between different sorts of trust. Occasionally investment trust shares trade at a premium to NAV.

The investment trust fan will counter by asking you to set the issue of NAV discounts to one side, and appreciate that an investment trust fund manager has much more control of the investment management. A unit trust fund manager, it will be argued, has to buy shares when new cash subscriptions from investors are received. Likewise, shares or other assets held in the unit trust have to be sold when unit holders want to withdraw. This obligation, according to the investment trustite, ties the unit trust fund manager's hands. He or she becomes a forced buyer or a forced seller. Timing of share purchases and sales is an important part of effective and profitable fund management, but the way a unit trust is structured takes control of that timing away from the fund manager.

The implication is that all unit holders may suffer if there is a rush to cash in units—for example at the time of a stock market crash. Elements of this kind of behaviour tarnished the image of unit trusts around Black Monday 1987.

The structure of a unit trust is simpler than for an investment trust. Money swills around a unit trust on one plane only. If cash comes in more assets are bought. If cash goes out, assets are sold. However, money washes around an investment trust on two planes. On one plane cash raised during the launch period is used to buy assets. These assets are then managed so that the original money is effectively invested and reinvested in accordance with predetermined objectives.

After the initial launch period it is as if the money earmarked for buying and selling underlying assets is separated from the hustle and bustle of investors' comings and goings. Investors becoming involved or leaving the fold after the launch period operate on a second plane. This secondary plane is where shares in the investment trust company change hands, through the Stock Exchange, and is the mechanism for new investors to replace old ones.

NAV OR NOT AN NAV

An investment trust commonly trades at a discount to the NAV. It therefore follows that it is rarely a good idea to take part in an investment trust launch, because the value of your investment is likely to drop.

There is a logical and an illogical reason why investment trust shares trade at a discount to NAV. The logical reason is that the NAV is only notional. The NAV of an investment trust share is based on the latest quoted price of investments held within the investment trust, not actual achievable market prices. If for any reason the assets were suddenly sold there is no guarantee that the notional values will be realised in a genuine trade. Investors in investment trust company shares, therefore, are not usually prepared to pay full notional value. In short, the second-hand market value is discounted by uncertainty.

The illogical reason is sentiment. Sentiment—a purely human emotion—is enormously important in the operation of any market but is particularly powerful in stock market mechanics. A market, after all, is only a collection of people, people who behave differently, people who are different, and who have different objectives and ways of operating.

Sentiment is not necessarily a rational force; a buyer of shares may pay over the odds because he is happy, because it is a sunny day, because he has a positive hunch, because—well because of almost anything you care to mention. Similarly a seller may accept a low price because he is feeling well disposed. Of course, the opposite is also true: unreasonably hard bargains might be negotiated because investors got out of bed the wrong side that morning.

Peter Walls, investment trust analyst at the leading London stockbroker Credit Lyonnais Laing, is one of the leading experts in the field. If anyone can explain discount to NAV he should be able to. Yet even he admitted to me—in generalisation—'There is no real rhyme or reason why discounts persist. They just do.'

Unit trust fans will point to the phenomenon of investment trust NAV discounts and suggest this makes investment trusts less attractive. True, the NAV problem means there are two performance measures which need to be monitored: the investment trust share price and the NAV per share. Both can vary, a fact which compounds the uncertainty in the investment. However, you can also look at NAV discounts positively. If you buy an investment trust company's shares at a price below NAV you may be buying those assets cheaply. Additionally, if the discount narrows you make money on the shares even if the actual NAV remains static. Investment trust firms work hard to keep the NAV discount at a minimum and investors can benefit if strategy or chance works to narrow the gap. But investors can also suffer if the NAV discount gap widens.

The gap between an investment trust company's share price and its NAV tends to be widest in **bear markets**, and narrowest in **bull markets**. This is because market sentiment—the force of which can rarely be underestimated—is positive towards investment companies in the good times and negative in the bad. However, many other factors can influence the degree of discount and even the most ardent investment trust advocate would have to admit that an investor who sets out to ride narrowing discounts will probably need more luck than judgement.

bear market: negative stock market conditions.

bull market: positive stock market conditions.

SOMETHING BORROWED

The structure of an investment trust has another important implication. Like other companies, it can borrow money. A unit trust cannot do this.

If it borrows money it can buy more assets in the form of shares, bonds, property or whatever. This in turn means that the potential for profit is greater. It also means that there is more room for loss. Companies—like investment trusts—which borrow money are said to take on '**gearing**', or to become 'leveraged'. The meaning behind both terms, the former of which is UK parlance while the other is more commonly used in the USA, becomes self-explanatory when you understand that borrowed money has a magnifying effect. Borrowing money can mean profits are increased, but also that losses can be deepened.

gearing: the amount of money a company borrows expressed as a percentage of its net assets.

The ability to borrow money is very helpful if used wisely. Foreign & Colonial (F&C), the oldest investment fund operator, is proud of its decision to borrow money in late 1974 and early 1975. It used the extra money to increase investment in equities, just when the prices seemed to be falling to alarmingly low levels and nearly to a point where complete financial meltdown was anticipated. It was a brave decision, but one which paid off because hindsight informs us that equity prices recovered. With hindsight we can see that F&C bought equities cheaply. By borrowing money it was able to buy more of the cheap assets and its overall investment performance was enhanced.

Investment trusts which borrow money have to pay interest on that money of course, and any returns on the investments bought with that borrowed money will be diminished by interest paid on the loans. It is clearly only sensible to borrow money to invest if anticipated returns exceed the cost of the borrowing. Anticipated returns should also provide compensation for the risk that the investment, on borrowed money, turns sour.

Official documents published by an investment trust should outline its policy on borrowing. Half-year and full-year reports may volunteer the information openly, otherwise you will have to work it out from the numbers provided.

The debt figure will appear on the balance sheet—the document which gives a snapshot picture of any company's total wealth. But the actual, absolute, amount of borrowing taken on by an investment trust company does not really mean very much. What, after all, is the definition of a large—or indeed a small—amount of debt? Is it £50,000? £5 million? £500 million?

Debt levels, like so many numbers, only really have relevance when they are put in suitable context. The appropriate context for a company's debt position is its asset position. If a company's assets are £1 million, £50,000 of debt is not very much. As a proportion of assets, debt is only 5%. But if the company has assets of £1 million and borrowings of £5 million the tables are turned and justifiable doubts about the stability of the finances could be raised.

It is debt expressed as a proportion of assets which is called gearing and gearing is usually expressed as a percentage. Generally, prudent trust managers would not want to take on debts greater than 15–20% of assets. Special circumstances may justify higher debts levels. Some investment trust companies may choose not to borrow at all.

MARKETING

There is one other difference between unit and investment trusts worth mentioning here, and it centres on marketing. The two types of investment fund are sold in quite different ways.

There is an old saying about insurance, and it applies to a lesser extent to investment funds: it is never bought, always sold. Unit trusts are predominantly sold by agents working for the unit trust management company. These agents are sometimes tied to one particular provider (and are called **tied agents**) or are independent financial advisers (IFAs) able to sell unit trusts from any source. But irrespective of whether an agent is tied or independent he or she is usually paid by commission. This commission is paid directly from the sums invested, and is a clear motivating force for advisers to promote this type of investment fund.

Investment trusts, on the other hand, are the favoured investment fund type among stockbrokers. This reality may not be unrelated to the fact that stockbrokers earn their living by commissions and fees levied when shares are traded and investing in an investment trust means buying an investment trust company share.

The separate channels of distribution have vested interests associated with them. But the real issues do not centre on whether a unit trust or investment trust is better. Rather, the important decision to make is which of a very broad range of

tied agent: a financial adviser employed to sell the investment products of one company only. Most investment sales people in high street banks and building societies are tied agents. Independent financial advisers – IFAs – have freedom to recommend all companies products.

funds—from either camp—is best suited to a investor's need to build savings, to protect them from inflation, and to meet the challenges of future financial security.

Some sales of both unit trusts and investment trusts are made direct to consumers, and this is a developing trend. This is an increasingly attractive option for many because they do not trust the advice offered by advisers or stockbrokers. Dealing direct can lessen charges, too.

Another difference between unit and investment trusts concerns the rules on advertising. Investment trusts, as companies, are not allowed to advertise the attractions of buying their shares. If they were, according to the logic, it could create a false market in the value of the shares. The price of a share ought to relate to the underlying operating and profit performance, not the skill or determination of marketing departments. Advertising creates demand and because an investment trust company's shares are in limited supply the advertising-led demand could lead to false price rises. A unit trust has no such obligations and the open ended structure means it is less constricted. But as a result of the fact that unit trusts can advertise themselves, they have grown more quickly, and have grown larger.

Different rules on the way unit and investment trusts advertise do not impact on the structure of either kind of investment fund but do go some way to explain why the amount of money in unit trusts (about £120 billion at the last count) is so much greater than for investment trusts where there is £55 billion.

(Investment trusts do advertise, but they cannot directly encourage people to buy the shares. What they do do, however, is advertise their financial performance or perhaps a savings scheme attached to the trust. Purists may say advertising of any sort could create false demand which in turn may disadvantage all shareholders. It is an arguable point.)

OEICS

Since 1995 a new breed of investment fund has appeared on the scene, called the open-ended investment company, or OEIC. The phonetic spelling is 'Oik', which is amusing only if it makes the stuffier investment fund promoters and regulators squirm with discomfort.

The unit trust side of the investment fund family has claimed OEICs as their own, because they share an open-ended structure. In truth they are something of a crossbreed and are similar to the majority of investment funds operational in North America and other parts of the world. OEICs have come into being in Britain largely in an attempt to attract funds from overseas, where the OEIC-type framework is better known. States within the European Union also seem keen to standardise things.

The relevance for the average UK investor is probably minimal. OEICs will not replace unit trusts over anything like the foreseeable future and those that do appear will be marketed as investment funds, a term which blurs the technical distinctions in any event.

Ten Reasons to Invest in Collectives

1. YOU WANT TO GET INVOLVED WITH STOCK MARKET INVESTMENT BUT YOU DO NOT KNOW HOW

You are attracted by the returns that can be achieved by taking on the risks of stock market investment. You are adventurous enough to find the interest rate on your bank or building society deposit account derisory.

2. YOU WANT TO SEE THE VALUE OF A HARD-EARNED NEST EGG GROW

Allowing for inflation the average UK-based unit and investment trust has given an average annual return of about 10% over the last 25 years. The average annual interest rate on a £1000 building society deposit has been about 3%.

If inflation tracks the same path over the next 25 years as it has followed during the last quarter of a century you will need £719 in 2121 to buy what costs £100 today. Some economic forecasters believe that inflation will be lower in the coming years than it was in the past. Inflation rates in the last 25 years reached 24.9% and were usually in the 6–12% range. But even if inflation does fall, say to the 2 and 3% seen in recent years, the effect can be alarming over longer periods. Between 1945 and 1970 the annual rate of inflation never rose above 12% and was commonly in the 2–4% range. Yet even in that relatively low inflation environment it still cost £261 in 1970 what it took £100 to pay for in 1945.

There are many ways of making sure the value of your nest egg retains its true value through index-linking. But if you use a good collective investment vehicle you can beat inflation and enhance the buying power of your wealth.

3. YOU ARE BUYING A HOUSE

You can use an investment fund to repay the capital element of a home loan. Some lenders have formal schemes which take advantage of tax-friendly PEP regulations but the underlying PEP investment is commonly an investment fund. But be aware that if you select badly you could see the value of your savings reduced or wiped out and in the process you could endanger your home ownership rights.

You could also save for a deposit on a home loan using an investment fund although you should remember that collective investments are best held for years, not months. It is best to put down a deposit on a home loan. That way the chances of slipping into negative equity are reduced. You can also take advantage of substantially cheaper mortgage interest rates if you can put up a sizeable deposit.

By using an investment fund you may be able to save a larger deposit more quickly. Rather than stowing a little of your wage packet away in the building society put it in an investment fund. Because money generally grows in value faster in stock market type investments you could sensibly set up home months, if not years, sooner.

4. AS A PENSIONER YOU WANT TO BOOST YOUR MONTHLY INCOME WHILE RETAINING THE VALUE OF YOUR CAPITAL

Retirement is meant to bring the golden age of leisure. Too often, however, it is filled with the constant worry that you will use up your savings in paying for everyday life. Careful use of an investment fund means you can preserve the value of your capital while drawing income at the same time.

5. USING INVESTMENT FUNDS AS A WAY TO CREATE A PENSION FUND

It is a relatively new concept, but several investment trust management companies—but not unit trust managers—have developed packaged products which channel pension contributions made through a working life into investment trusts. On retirement the investment trusts can be liquidated and part of the sum used to buy an annuity—a pension income providing vehicle.

Contributions made to an investment trust on this basis can be made out of untaxed income (up to certain limits). Investment profits earned before retirement also escape taxation. The advantages of investment trust pension plans above conventional pension-saving schemes are that charges on this kind of plan are cheap. It is also easy to see, monitor and possibly change the kind of investment trust where your pension savings are housed.

6. AS A GRANDPARENT YOU WANT TO SET ASIDE SOME MONEY FOR GRANDCHILDREN

You are well off enough to want to give some money away. You would rather hand some money down the generations than let the Inland Revenue relieve you of it by way of the dreaded inheritance tax.

But your grandchildren are young and have no need of anything more than pocket money. It would be nice to put a little something aside for their twenty-first birthday, but that is not for another 15 years or so. Using a collective, today's 'a little something' could be a substantial amount of cash when the time comes to put the key in the door.

7. YOU CAN SPARE A FEW POUNDS FROM YOUR MONTHLY SALARY CHEQUE AND WANT TO MAKE A COMMITMENT TO SAVING

It is all very well saying you will save for a rainy day, but unless you take the trouble to establish some kind of formal scheme you will never get round to it. And if you are like most people the few pounds you could set aside will end up disappearing.

Unit and investment trust savings schemes give you the discipline to act on your best intentions. That way maybe you will be able to afford a new car, take the holiday of a lifetime, buy a fitted kitchen and bathroom, give money away to charity. Money is a great facilitator, with it you can do or buy any one of a thousand things.

8. YOU HAVE NEITHER THE TIME NOR THE EXPERTISE TO INVEST DIRECTLY IN STOCK OR SHARES

If you use collective investment you can hitch your trailer to a truck driven by a full-time money manager. You have to choose a good manager and pay for the service of course, but at least you will be able to sleep easier at night knowing that your investment is being looked after by a professional.

9. YOU WANT TO PRESERVE AND MAKE THE MOST OF AN UNEXPECTED WINDFALL

Perhaps you have won on the National Lottery. Maybe you have a redundancy cheque and are lucky enough to find another job immediately. What happened to last year's Christmas bonus? Should you not try to hang on to at least some of it this year? Think about an investment fund.

10. YOU WANT TO SAVE UP FOR SCHOOL FEES

You would like to give your children the best education available but realise that the best is expensive. You fear that while your monthly salary will meet part of the cost it will not cover all of it.

Think about setting aside that spare element of salary before you actually have to spend the money. You can also maximise the value of thinking ahead by saving through some astutely chosen investment funds.

CHAPTER 5

Spoilt for Choice:
An Anatomy of Investment
Fund Types

The UK collective investment industry is crammed with more than 1600 unit trusts and 300 investment trusts. The bewildering array is categorised with some funds designed for people who want income, others for capital growth. Among other things funds are also set up to attract investors who want to invest in particular geographical areas or in particular industrial sectors, or who adopt an ethical stance.

This chapter is a step-by-step guide through the length and breadth of the market-place.

When it comes to selecting a particular unit or investment trust there is no shortage of choice. This is not only a bewildering array: it also means there are more collective investment vehicles than there are individual company shares quoted on the London Stock Exchange.

Fortunately the collective investment market-place is divided up into smaller and more manageable segments. Many of the funds are designed for people who want to buy exposure to shares and most investment funds aim to meet this demand.

Shares are the best understood way of investing in companies, but are not the only way. An increasing number of funds have bonds as the underlying investment. Some people use investment funds to access top bank deposit interest rates, others still use them to invest in property.

Some funds are set up to invest in a broad selection of different sorts of equities, bonds, bank deposits, property and the rest. Some are general, others are more specialised. Some are very specialised.

I have designed this chapter with the categorisation methods used by the two organisations which promote investment funds—the Association of Investment Trust Companies (AITC) and the Association of Unit Trusts and Investment Funds (AUTIF)—in mind. The AITC/AUTIF classification systems are used by statistics firms like Micropal in the preparation of performance tables.

Although the AITC and AUTIF classification systems share a great deal in common they are not exactly the same. Instead of choosing one or other system, I will profile the industry in a more general way, looking at the essential principles of each investment fund class irrespective of whether it is a unit trust or an investment trust. Hopefully it draws from the best in both the AUTIF and the AITC classification systems.

I am going to profile each grouping and suggest suitable groups of consumers. In addition, I have split the categorisation into three sections. The first profiles funds in terms of investment objectives. It will list the different varieties of fund as defined by underlying investment type. The second section features profiles of all the stock markets from around the world that private investors can get access to by using collective investment funds. It also looks at funds which invest in a mix of different markets. The third section profiles the more specialist funds,

funds which invest in smaller companies, the money market, split capital, commodities, energy and futures and options funds.

I have also roughly ordered the chapter so that the categories mentioned first are those designed to appeal to new investors, or investors who want the broadest exposure to the world's stock markets. Categories further down the list will appeal to those with more specialist requirements.

For some of the more popular fund types I include graphs showing 10 year performance accompanied by tables showing some of the best performing individual funds. The graphs show the best, worst and average performing funds. The tables name the top ten performing funds in the 10 year period to 1 August 1996. Some sectors are not large enough to sustain 10 funds, in which case all funds are shown. With the help of Micropal I also show how many funds exist in each category and the size of the sector in money terms. I also show a volatility measure where the higher the number the greater the volatility, and in many senses the higher the volatility the higher the risk profile.

Due to the time it takes for a book like this one to get from author's keyboard to reader's palm, the figures used will be out of date. But I include them because it will give some idea of the contrast in performance terms between different types of fund, and between different individually named funds within a sector. It will also introduce you to some of the top performing names to watch out for, although the list is in an inevitably constant state of flux.

My so-called Performance Monitors are not designed to be comprehensive, but simply to introduce the kind of information that investors should analyse. In a couple of cases—where available data has made this possible—I have included

Performance Monitors for both investment trusts and unit trusts.

For updated information private investors should buy *Money Management* magazine. *MM* is an independent monthly financial magazine published by the same company which publishes the *Financial Times*. It is primarily written for financial advisers but it provides one of the easiest and cheapest ways for private investors to find out about and monitor individual fund performance. It may take some time and effort accustoming yourself to the way the statistics are presented. To the beginner at first sight they look impenetrable, but they are in fact among the best set out and comprehensive performance charts. Micropal provides the statistics for *MM*.

MM is only stocked by large newsagents. For subscription enquiries write to PO Box 461, Bromley, Kent BR2 9WP or telephone 0181 402 8485.

SECTION 1: INVESTMENT STRATEGY

Managed Funds

Managed funds are the basic type and are sometimes called balanced funds. Managed funds use the money collected to invest in a bit of everything, in equities, **bonds**, bank deposits and other types of asset.

bond: a tradeable loan certificate issued by a government or a company. British government bonds are also called gilts.

Suitable investors

First time, cautious investors who want to advance their savings strategy beyond the bounds of the building society. An investor who wants a mix of equities and bonds to get exposure to the largest variety of different stock market instruments.

Equity General Funds

Most investment funds buy shares in trading companies. Shares and corporate bonds are similar in that both provide capital for a company; however, the similarities end there. A share has an indefinite life span, has an unlimited potential for growth in capital value, and holders are conferred with ownership rights to the issuing company. The ownership rights also mean that shareholders come bottom of the list when it comes to paying out creditors if a company is wound up. In other words, shares have an unlimited upside and an unlimited downside. The value of a share varies according to the state of a company's business and financial health. Market sentiment—mentioned in Chapter 3—also plays an important part. It is both the actual and the perceived strengths and weaknesses that determine the price of a share.

Dividends are paid to shareholders, usually twice a year. The income stream is another factor which helps set the market price of a share, but a large number of shares—particularly in small and growing companies, and in firms based in emerging countries in the Far East and Latin America—either pay nominal dividends or no dividends at all. They depend on their credentials for delivering capital growth to underpin the share price, and will say they need all the profit earned (from where dividend payments are funded) for investment in the business.

One of the most basic forms of equity investment fund is the general fund which invests in the widest range of different companies' shares. General funds invest in large companies and small companies. They also invest in the shares of companies from a wide range of industries—from mining to insurance, retailing to pharmaceuticals. They may also invest across a spread of different geographical locations, in companies which pay good dividends and in firms that concentrate on delivering advancing capital values.

Because general funds are the broadest based of equity investment funds their performance is among the most reliable, when compared to other investment fund categories. Reliable, but not spectacular. Statisticians at Micropal split unit trusts into 25 categories. Over the last 3, 5 and 10 years UK equity general funds are consistently ranked between twelfth and seventeenth. General funds are also among the most popular. Micropal estimates that there is £20 billion invested in general funds, about 15% of the total.

It is a similar story for investment trusts. Funds in UK equity general investment trusts sector total £1.8 billion and performance, in the context of investment funds, is steady rather than inspired.

Suitable investors

Relatively unambitious investors who want to reap the all-round benefits of equity investment. People who want to earn returns from the rise in the capital value of shares and to receive dividend income.

Capital Growth Funds

There are two ways of making money out of equities. The best known is to hope that the capital value of shares increases but companies also pay dividends to shareholders, dividends which provide income. General funds and balanced funds invest with the aim of reaping both kinds of reward.

However, investors can specialise and buy into funds which concentrate on shares where the prospects for share price increases are good. These funds are called capital growth funds, and suit more adventurous investors, and younger investors.

Capital growth investors also need more patience: it takes time for the benefits of a capital growth strategy to materialise. Five years is a sensible minimum, although you could be lucky and earn handsome rewards in time periods shorter than that. The best and most reliable returns are earned over periods of 10 years and more.

Broadly based capital growth funds invest across the range of different types of companies. As a rule, however, they target younger companies who sell products or services to new and expanding market-places. Another constituency for capital growth funds are companies which have lived through a bad patch but are recovering.

Suitable investors

Investors with a longer-term view, and who are prepared to countenance greater risk in return for potentially greater rewards – see Performance Monitors 1 and 2.

Income Funds

Income funds concentrate on the other side of the coin, buying shares in companies where the dividend payments are generous. Other income funds invest in equities and bonds. Bonds are valued for the income they pay.

Any company can decide to pay generous dividends. However, it is usual for companies which operate in mature market-places to compensate investors for the lack of potential share price growth with a good dividend. Shares in utility companies— like the privatised water and electricity companies —are the kind typically bought by income funds. If you invest in income funds you can elect to draw income, monthly, quarterly, half-yearly or annually. Or you could choose to have the income roll up in

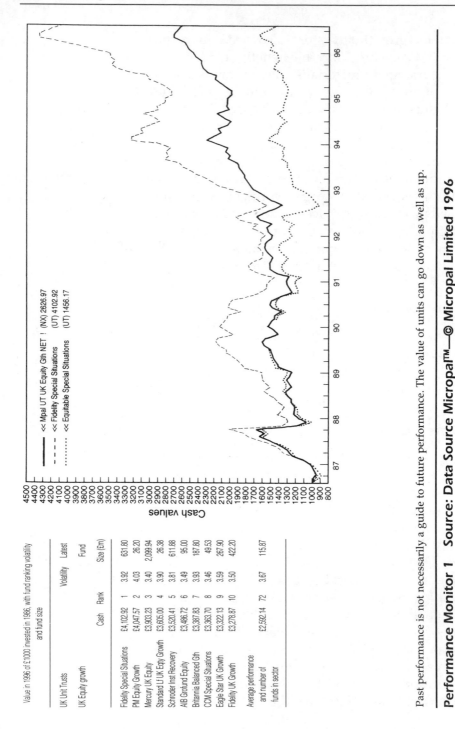

Value in 1996 of £1000 invested in 1996, with fund ranking volatility and fund size

UK Unit Trusts	Cash	Rank	Volatility	Latest Fund Size (£m)
UK Equity growth				
Fidelity Special Situations	£4,102.92	1	3.92	631.80
PM Equity Growth	£4,047.57	2	4.03	26.20
Mercury UK Equity	£3,903.23	3	3.40	2,099.94
Standard Lf UK Eqty Growth	£3,605.00	4	3.90	26.38
Schroder Inst Recovery	£3,520.41	5	3.81	611.88
AIB Grofund Equity	£3,498.72	6	3.49	95.00
Britannia Balanced Gth	£3,387.83	7	3.93	187.80
CCM Special Situations	£3,363.70	8	3.46	49.53
Eagle Star UK Growth	£3,322.13	9	3.59	267.90
Fidelity UK Growth	£3,278.87	10	3.50	422.20
Average performance and number of funds in sector	£2,592.14	72	3.67	115.87

<< Mpal UT UK Equity Gth NET !   (NX) 2626.97
<< Fidelity Special Situations   (UT) 4102.92
<< Equitable Special Situations (UT) 1456.17

Cash values

Past performance is not necessarily a guide to future performance. The value of units can go down as well as up.

Performance Monitor 1   Source: Data Source Micropal™—© Micropal Limited 1996

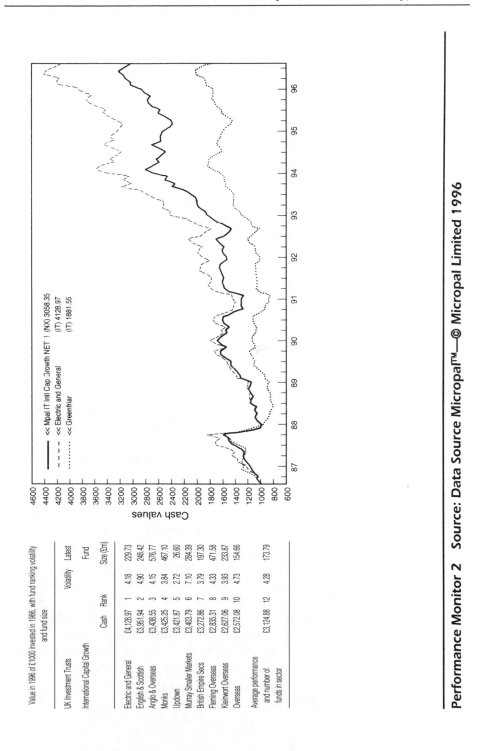

UK Investment Trusts	Volatility		Latest
International Capital Growth			Fund
	Cash	Rank	Size (£m)
Electric and General	£4,128.97	1	4.18	229.73
English & Scottish	£3,951.94	2	4.90	248.42
Anglo & Overseas	£3,438.55	3	4.15	576.77
Monks	£3,425.25	4	3.84	467.10
Updown	£3,421.87	5	2.72	26.60
Murray Smaller Markets	£3,403.79	6	7.10	284.39
British Empire Secs	£3,272.86	7	3.79	197.30
Fleming Overseas	£2,835.31	8	4.33	471.58
Kleinwort Overseas	£2,627.06	9	3.93	233.87
Overseas	£2,572.08	10	4.73	154.66
Average performance and number of funds in sector	£3,124.88	12	4.28	173.79

Value in 1996 of £1,000 invested in 1986, with fund ranking volatility and fund size

Cash values

<< Mpal IT Int'l Cap Growth NET ! (NX) 3058.35
<< Electric and General (IT) 4128.97
<< Greenfriar (IT) 1881.55

Performance Monitor 2   Source: Data Source Micropal™—© Micropal Limited 1996

the fund by leaving instructions that dividend income should be constantly reinvested.

It is interesting to notice that while the investment strategy between equity growth and income funds is fundamentally different the actual performance is not. Among investment trusts the average one-year performance of a capital growth fund to 1 March 1996 was +22%. Using comparable figures the equivalent average income fund grew by exactly the same amount. In the unit trust sector the average capital growth fund rose by 68% in the five years to 29 March 1996, and the equivalent income fund grew by 58% in the same period. Across 10 years the average UK capital growth unit trust grew +161% while the income equivalent grew +183%.

Suitable investors

Pensioners and other investors who have a lump sum and need to draw an income to finance everyday expenditure. Also those who believe that if a company pays good dividends it will be attractive to many shareholders and therefore the capital value of shares will rise – see Performance Monitors 3 and 4.

Note: Income-seeking investors ought to be aware of one of the investment community's oldest and favourite tricks: that is, to pay income out of capital. If an income is maintained at a certain level at the expense of capital, you may find the value of a nest egg is quickly eroded.

A vicious circle becomes established where less capital is available from which to generate the predetermined level of income. So more capital is used to maintain income, making it even more difficult to generate the original level of income from ongoing investment.

Be especially wary of guarantees. These are exceptionally difficult for financial firms to set up, and almost invariably involve some sort of catch. The catch may not be serious and as long as you are aware of how a guarantee works, the product may work in your favour overall. A guarantee is only as good as its guarantor.

Ethical Investment

If you hold strong ideological views you may be put off stock market investment because it implies the provision of financial support to companies involved in politically incorrect activities. However, a sizeable number of investment managers now operate funds specifically designed for those who want to invest in the stock market, but avoid companies involved in ethically unsound or environmentally unfriendly lines of business. Green funds usually avoid companies which are involved in the manufacture, distribution and sale of armaments, alcohol, tobacco products, pornography, and chemical pollutants. However, the precise investment criteria differ from one individual fund to another.

Investing with scruples makes investment much harder work. Some of Britain's biggest and most successful companies are tainted: GEC, Guinness, BAT Industries and Hanson are out for a start. But ethical investment has proved it can deliver results too.

The oldest established green fund, called the Stewardship Fund and run by the Friends Provident investment house, comes a respectable twentieth out of 69 UK equity growth funds in existence for the last 10 years. An investment of £100 over that period would have turned into £282. It seems you have to be even more patient with green investments than with most others because the

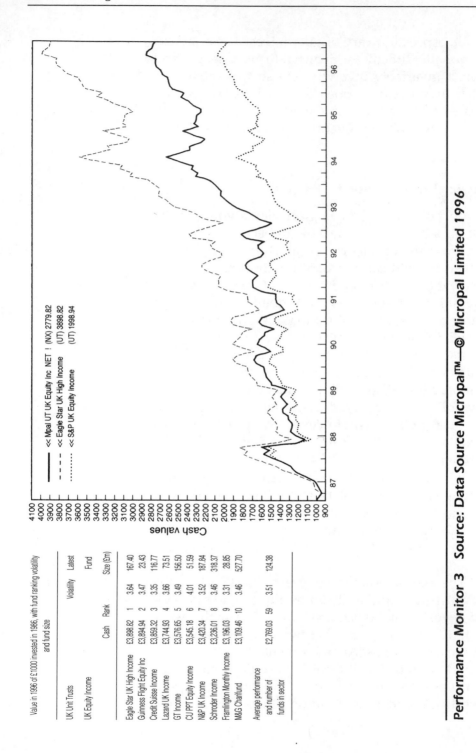

Value in 1996 of £1000 invested in 1986, with fund ranking volatility and fund size

UK Unit Trusts		Volatility	Latest
UK Equity Income			Fund
	Cash	Rank	Size (£m)
Eagle Star UK High Income	£3,898.82	1	3.64	167.40
Guinness Flight Equity Inc	£3,894.94	2	3.47	23.43
Credit Suisse Income	£3,859.32	3	3.35	116.77
Lazard UK Income	£3,744.93	4	3.66	73.51
GT Income	£3,576.65	5	3.49	156.50
CU PPT Equity Income	£3,545.18	6	4.01	51.59
N&P UK Income	£3,420.34	7	3.52	187.84
Schroder Income	£3,236.01	8	3.46	318.37
Framlington Monthly Income	£3,196.03	9	3.31	28.85
M&G Charifund	£3,109.46	10	3.46	527.70
Average performance and number of funds in sector	£2,769.03	59	3.51	124.38

Cash values

87 88 89 90 91 92 93 94 95 96

<< Mpal UT UK Equity Inc NET ! (NX) 2779.82
<< Eagle Star UK High Income   (UT) 3898.82
<< S&P UK Equity Income   (UT) 1998.94

Performance Monitor 3   Source: Data Source Micropal™—© Micropal Limited 1996

Value in 1996 of £1000 invested in 1986, with fund ranking volatility and fund size

	Cash	Rank	Volatility	Latest Fund Size (£m)
UK Unit Trusts				
UK Equity & Bond Income				
N&P Higher Income	£3,023.38	1	3.32	39.92
CU PPT High Yield	£2,858.09	2	3.76	39.23
Prolific Extra Income	£2,831.59	3	3.07	148.60
HTR Extra Income	£2,698.87	4	3.16	61.40
INVESCO UK Extra Income	£2,404.35	5	3.30	65.80
Edinburgh High Distribution	£2,378.93	6	3.66	14.70
Gartmore High Income	£2,233.08	7	3.19	55.43
Midland High Yield	£2,207.67	8	2.94	42.90
Prudential High Income	£2,123.91	9	3.00	22.20
Friends Prov Monthly Dist	£1,965.28	10	2.91	17.41
Average performance and number of funds in sector	£2,423.48	11	3.04	64.20

Legend:

<< Mpal UT UK Eqty & Bd Inc NET ! (NX) 2549.63
<< N&P Higher Income (UT) 3023.38
<< Midland Extra High Income (UT) 1933.13

Cash values

Performance Monitor 4   Source: Data Source Micropal™—© Micropal Limited 1996

Stewardship's relative performance worsens over shorter past periods.

Suitable investors

People who want to invest with their heart as well as their mind.

Tracker Funds

An increasingly popular type of equity fund is the tracker fund, so-called because it is designed to track the performance of a relevant index. Since many investors judge the performance of a particular fund manager against a benchmark index many fund managers see little point in attempting to outperform the index because of the risk that underperformance may result.

Tracker funds buy all the shares included in an index, or a representative sample, and benchmark performance is assured. For example an FTSE 100 index tracker buys shares in each of Britain's largest 100 companies.

Tracker funds have the added advantage that very little specialist professional management expertise is required in order to achieve the goals set. In fact, a computer can do it. The advantage is that this makes tracker funds cheap to manage and investors draw the benefit in lower fees. Lower fees automatically mean better performance and in some cases the increased performance achieved by lower fees could be higher than the outperformance generated by specialist stock selection.

Tracker funds are ideal for novice investors because the investment aims are thoroughly transparent. If you appreciate that, say, the FTSE 100 index produces better returns than the building society you need to do no more than buy an FTSE 100 index tracking investment fund. You do not need to be able to appreciate the finer differences between investment management companies. Within reason any old firm will do—although you ought to check that anyone who offers to look after your money has proper and official regulatory accreditation.

Investing in a tracker means surrendering the opportunity to secure outstanding returns but it does mean you avoid disappointing ones. It is also easy to monitor the performance of your money invested in a tracker. Movements in the FTSE 100 index are widely reported in newspapers, and in radio and television news bulletins, making it easier to monitor the health of your investment.

Investment is safer if you approach the task with a good helping of realism and cynicism. Ask yourself questions: What makes an investment manager so special that he can achieve above-average performance? Is it not better to have average performance and peace of mind? Exposure to the possibility of above-average performance means you are also exposed to the threat of seeing below-average returns.

One thing you do need to be careful about, however, is that the tracker fund management company does not siphon off all the dividend income from equities in the portfolio. A tracker only really tracks an index's performance if it tracks the capital and income elements of performance. Does the fund declare that the income from the shares will be reinvested in your fund?

Suitable investors

Novice investors who want to learn more about stock market investment. Trackers do not take the risk out of equity investment and it is worth remembering that they track an index down as well as up. But they do allow investors to avoid worse than average performance. Bear in mind that you can buy into funds which track any one of a number of indices, not just UK measures. Trackers may be a good way to dip a toe in the French, North American or Japanese markets.

SECTION 2: WORLD STOCK MARKETS

International Funds

International unit and investment trusts are, in geographical terms, the most broadly spread of all collective funds. Most are defined as those which have less than 80% of their assets in any one geographical area. In practice international funds buy shares in the companies of the world's major industrialised countries: the UK, the USA and Japan.

International funds also tend to buy shares in those countries' biggest companies. Companies from the UK are likely to be listed among the top 100—member of the *Financial Times*/Stock Exchange 100 index (commonly known as the Footsie index). Shares from the USA may well be constituents of the Dow Jones Industrial Average and in Japan shares bought will probably be members of the Nikkei 225. International fund managers should select the promising company shares from the most promising stock markets.

In the early to mid 1990s the USA was a rapidly rising market and Japan was the poor performer while the UK came somewhere in between. Clearly, the best performing funds in that period are the ones which owned shares predominantly of US origin. The poorest performers will be those which put faith in Japan. However, the USA will not always be the promising place to invest just as Japan will not be a permanent inhabitant of the doldrums. The art of good investment management is being able to spot which markets have the potential to rise and which are likely to fall. Profit comes from accurately predicting future trends.

Investment managers can and do get it wrong. Many UK fund managers pulled out of the USA at the start of 1995 believing that the general price of shares over there might fall. In the event the benchmark equity market index rose by just under 40% in the year.

International funds do not have to restrict themselves to the world's largest stock markets. Indeed many invest in stock markets of countries all around the globe to give the fund a truly international flavour. However, as a tribe international funds are cautious and the biggest, most well-established stock markets suit them because they are also the most dependable. There is safety in size, and an individual country's stock market reflects the state and strength of that country's economy.

Suitable investors

Those new to collectives but who want to use them for exposure to shares and so have a developed appetite for risk. Within this category of investors who want equities, however, international funds are suited to those people with a more cautious temperament, those who want the broadest exposure to the broadest number of stock markets around the world – see Performance Monitor 5.

UK Funds

An investment fund specialising in the UK stock market is where most UK investors start. There is one illogical, though thoroughly understandable reason for this, and one very logical reason. The illogical reason why many UK investors stick to UK funds is that it means supporting the home team. The understandable, emotional, urge is to back UK companies. Buy British and all that.

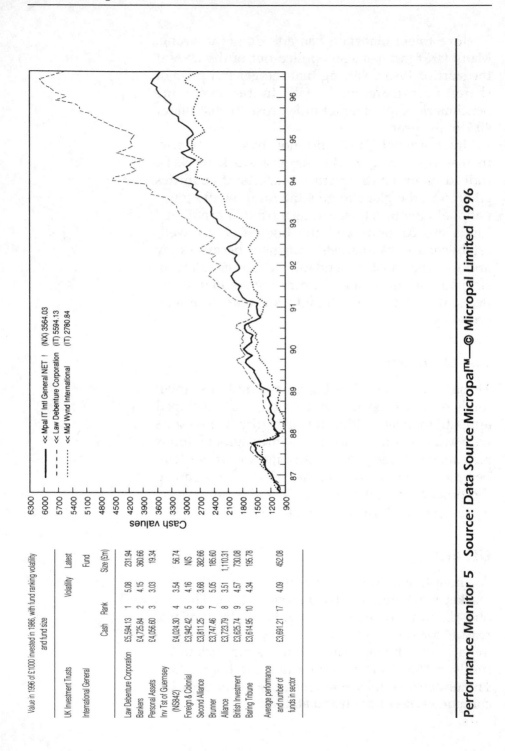

Performance Monitor 5   Source: Data Source Micropal™—© Micropal Limited 1996

The logical reason to buy British is that if you are British and you invest in British companies you do not expose yourself to dangers in the currency exchange markets. Exchange rates can, and often do, fluctuate wildly. When former UK Chancellor Norman Lamont surrendered sterling's position in the European exchange rate mechanism (ERM) the pound slumped in value compared to practically every currency in the world. More recently, at the end of 1994, the Mexican peso took a chastising bath. Less dramatic movements, however, are happening all the time. The relationship between UK pounds and US dollars is relatively stable. But as Figure 5.1 shows, that is not saying much. During the past 15 years £100 has bought as few as $100 or as many as $200.

Figure 5.1   £/$ exchange rate. Source: Datastream. Reproduced by permission of Datastream International

Working through the effect of currencies induces brain ache in the brightest of people, but the impact of exchange rates can be enormous. Imagine you bought £100 worth of shares in a US company when the exchange rate was £1 to $1. If you sold those same shares when the exchange rate had moved to £1 to $2, but the share price had stayed the same, the value of your investment would have dropped to £50. And that is before you take account of any management charges or dealing fees.

Swings as wide as that are rare. But the more money you invest the greater the impact of smaller exchange rate movements. Imagine you invested £100,000 in US shares when £100 bought $140. At the outset your investment would be worth $140,000. However, if the currencies markets moved so that £100 bought $160 the value of your US investment, in terms of pounds sterling, would be cut from £100,000 to £87,500.

Even a small change in exchange rates can make a big difference. Vagaries of currencies can wipe out hard-won investment gains with worrying ease. Currencies can work to your advantage, of course: like most things to do with investment there are two sides to the story. But forecasting exchange rate movements is a notoriously thankless task. It is a good deal trickier than forecasting what will happen to share prices, and that is tricky enough. Investing in UK funds means you avoid the worry about exchange rates.

There will always be some currency risk if you invest overseas, although this can be kept to a minimum if you choose a broadly based international fund. If investments are spread in a host of different countries the chances are that the combined effect of all the exchange rate movements—some going one way, some the other—will cancel each other out.

There is a third reason to invest in UK-based funds and that is because you believe that UK stocks and shares represent value for money and you think there is every chance that the value of your investment will rise – see Performance Monitor 6.

Suitable investors

UK funds are another place for newcomers. UK general, UK balanced or UK tracker funds are where complete novices can start the stock market familiarisation process. With a UK fund there is also the chance that you will recognise some of the companies in which the investment fund invests.

During this learning process it is best to stick with UK funds—unless there is a good reason not to. That way you avoid the added complication of the foreign exchange market.

North American Funds

The biggest stock market in the world is in New York. The total combined value of listed US and Canadian company shares is more than all the rest of the world put together. The US economy is strong and largely self-sufficient. The North American population is an enormous market of consumers; it has plentiful oil and mineral resources; a broad spread of industrial and service companies thrive there; and its people are well educated and innovative.

Investment funds specialising in North America are popular in the UK. There are 150 North American unit and investment trusts with £6 billion of assets, making it one of the largest investment fund subsectors. North American funds usually invest in companies quoted on the New York Stock Exchange, but the NYSE does not have a monopoly. There are many other exchanges.

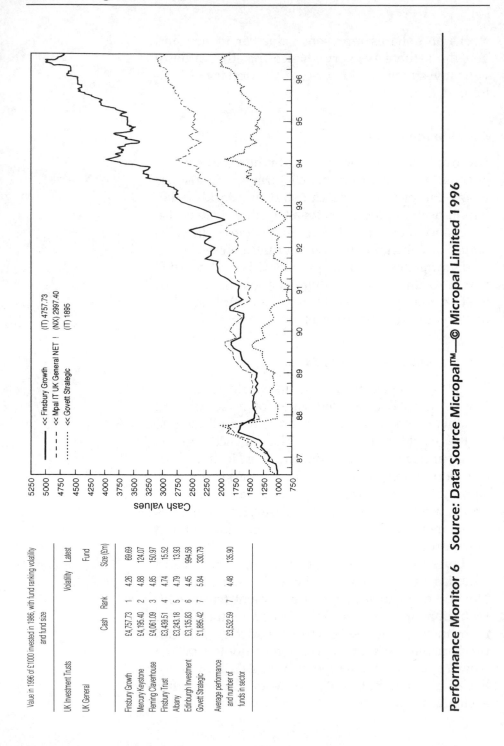

Value in 1996 of £1000 invested in 1996, with fund ranking volatility and fund size

UK Investment Trusts	Cash	Rank	Volatility	Latest Fund Size (£m)
UK General				
Finsbury Growth	£4,757.73	1	4.26	69.69
Mercury Keystone	£4,195.40	2	4.88	124.07
Fleming Claverhouse	£4,061.09	3	4.85	150.97
Finsbury Trust	£3,439.51	4	4.74	15.52
Albany	£3,243.18	5	4.79	13.93
Edinburgh Investment	£3,135.63	6	4.45	994.58
Govett Strategic	£1,895.42	7	5.84	330.79
Average performance and number of funds in sector	£3,532.59	7	4.48	135.90

Performance Monitor 6   Source: Data Source Micropal™—© Micropal Limited 1996

The best known exchange apart from NYSE is called Nasdaq. The acronym stands for National Association of Stock Dealers Automated Quotation. Nasdaq is not based in any one particular place, but exists electronically across America. Companies quoted on Nasdaq are usually smaller. It also has an international dimension: companies from the UK and elsewhere which want to attract North American investors commonly obtain a Nasdaq listing.

Suitable investors

Big, in investment terms, is usually beautiful so if you fancy a little specialisation and adventure overseas, look at North America first. But be mindful that even the largest markets fall, and North America is no exception. It is important to look for value for money – see Performance Monitor 7.

Europe including the UK

The search for stock markets which are undervalued is the holy grail to professional investment managers. Private investors who want more than the very basic benefits from stock market investment have to embark on the same journey. Chapter 10 outlines basic investment management and analysis techniques. Some or all of these techniques should be employed when making a decision about investing in overseas funds.

European funds including the UK are perhaps a first step for the fledgling investor because, as with international funds, overseas exposure is combined with investment in the UK. The narrow definition of a Europe-wide unit or investment trust is one with no more than 80% of its assets in the shares of one country.

To have 80% of money in one market, however, rather defeats the object of a pan-Europe fund

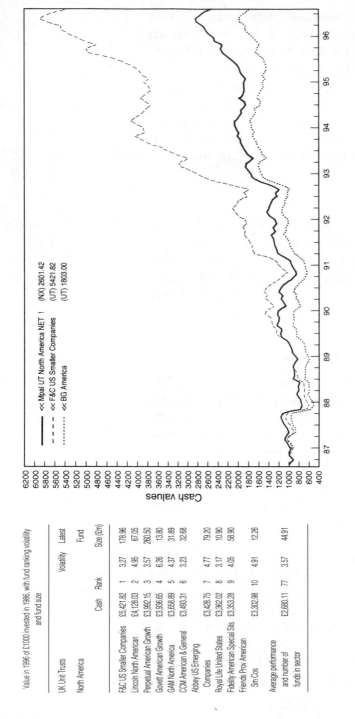

Value in 1996 of £1000 invested in 1986, with fund ranking volatility and fund size

UK Unit Trusts		Volatility	Latest
North America			Fund
	Cash	Rank	Size (£m)
F&C US Smaller Companies	£5,421.82	1	3.27	178.96
Lincoln North American	£4,128.03	2	4.95	67.05
Perpetual American Growth	£3,992.15	3	3.57	260.50
Govett American Growth	£3,936.65	4	6.26	13.80
GAM North America	£3,658.89	5	4.37	31.89
CCM American & General	£3,493.31	6	3.23	32.68
Abbey US Emerging Companies	£3,428.75	7	4.77	79.20
Royal Life United States	£3,362.02	8	3.17	10.90
Fidelity American Special Sits	£3,353.28	9	4.05	58.90
Friends Prov American Sm Cos	£3,302.98	10	4.91	12.26
Average performance and number of funds in sector	£2,680.11	77	3.57	44.91

Legend for chart:

—— << Mpal UT North America NET !   (NX) 2601.42
- - - - << F&C US Smaller Companies   (UT) 5421.82
· · · · · · · · · << BG America   (UT) 1803.00

Cash values axis: 6200, 6000, 5800, 5600, 5400, 5200, 5000, 4800, 4600, 4400, 4200, 4000, 3800, 3600, 3400, 3200, 3000, 2800, 2600, 2400, 2200, 2000, 1800, 1600, 1400, 1200, 1000, 800, 600, 400

Years: 87, 88, 89, 90, 91, 92, 93, 94, 95, 96

Performance Monitor 7   Source: Data Source Micropal™—© Micropal Limited 1996

which is to spread money around in order to glean benefits from as many markets as possible and also reduce the impact of a disappointment or two. In practice, fund managers will spread investment around with large portions of a trust's assets invested in the major markets—London, Frankfurt, Paris and Amsterdam—with lesser amounts in smaller bourses.

It is useful for the investment manager to have the option to keep as much as 80% in a single market in case something unpleasant is threatened and money needs to find a safe haven.

The 80% rule is only general. Each individual fund will be established under an individual set of rules. Investors should pay special attention to the section in a investment firm's literature which explains investment aims and criteria. Investment reports after 6 and 12 months also give useful information about the investment tactics being employed on your behalf.

It is fair to note at this point that while the pan-Europe funds do spread investment around to maximise investment potential and minimise investment risk most of the European bourses move in tandem. Many European nations, particularly those in the European Union, trade closely with each other. In addition quite a few currencies informally shadow the strong German mark, and look to the German economy for leadership in other monetary and financial affairs such as the setting of interest rates.

Suitable investors

If you think European companies—compared to Japanese or US firms—hold promise a pan-Europe fund might be for you. Investors must be prepared for greater risk, and be able to stomach higher management fees, justified by the more difficult tasks managers have to perform to find out about and acquire overseas stocks – see Performance Monitor 8.

Europe Excluding the UK

These are sometimes called Continental European funds. Much of what was said about Europe funds including the UK applies here. The important difference is that investors do not have the safety blanket of knowing that the UK market, the most sophisticated and best established of the European markets, is acting as long stop. As such these funds are higher risk, but are potentially more rewarding too.

Suitable investors

Europe funds are the most specialist mentioned so far. Investors should have a quite firm idea of what they expect from a European fund, and be aware that the risks—compared to a broadly based UK or international fund—are significant.

A European investment fund should not be a core investment. It should account for no more than about 10–20% of the total amount of money saved in an investment portfolio. A Europe fund might be held in conjunction with a UK fund or two, an international fund and some individual shares—perhaps bought in a privatisation issue. A well-spread portfolio would include some gilts—UK government loans—other corporate bonds and, in case of emergency, something put by in a bank or building society deposit too – see Performance Monitor 9.

Japan Funds

After North America, the most important market is probably Japan although it is a pretty close call with London.

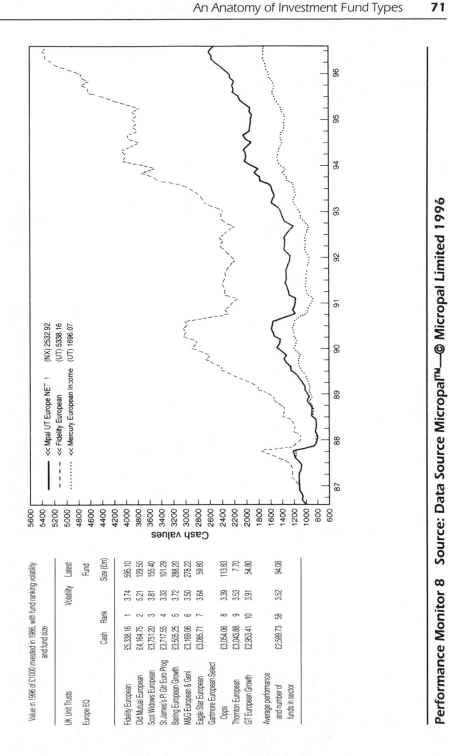

Europe EQ	Cash Rank	Volatility	Latest Fund Size (£m)
Fidelity European	1	3.74	595.10
Old Mutual European	2	5.21	129.50
Scot Widows European	3	3.81	155.40
St.James's Pl Gtr Euro Prog	4	3.33	101.29
Baring European Growth	5	3.72	288.20
M&G European & Genl	6	3.50	278.22
Eagle Star European	7	3.64	59.80
Gartmore European Select Opps	8	3.39	113.83
Thornton European	9	3.53	7.70
GT European Growth	10	3.91	54.80
Average performance and number of funds in sector	58	3.52	94.08

Value in 1996 of £1000 invested in 1986, with fund ranking volatility and fund size

UK Unit Trusts · Volatility · Latest Fund Size (£m)

Cash values : 5338.16 (Fidelity European) ... 2599.73

Legend:
<< Mpal UT Europe NET   (NX) 2532.92
<< Fidelity European   (UT) 5338.16
<< Mercury European Income (UT) 1696.07

Performance Monitor 8 Source: Data Source Micropal™—© Micropal Limited 1996

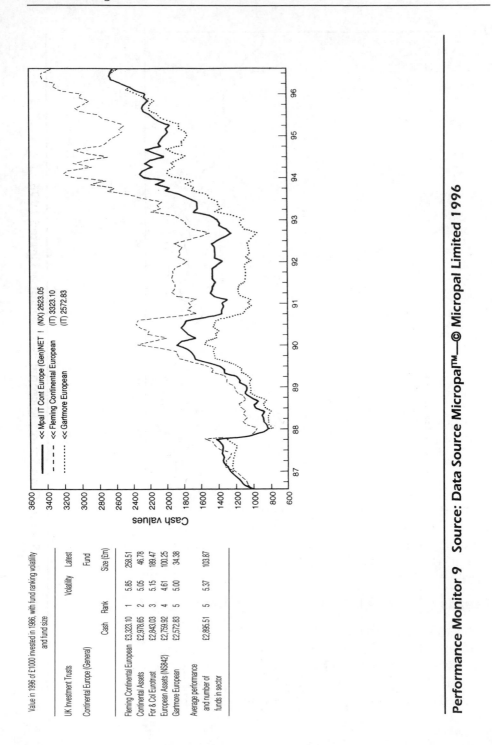

Value in 1996 of £1000 invested in 1996, with fund ranking volatility and fund size				
UK Investment Trusts		Volatility	Latest	Fund
Continental Europe (General)				
	Cash	Rank		Size (£m)
Fleming Continental European	£3,323.10	1	5.85	258.51
Continental Assets	£2,978.65	2	5.05	46.78
For & Col Eurotrust	£2,843.03	3	5.15	189.47
European Assets (NS842)	£2,759.92	4	4.61	100.25
Gartmore European	£2,572.83	5	5.00	34.38
Average performance and number of funds in sector	£2,895.51	5	5.37	103.87

<< Mpal IT Cont Europe (Gen)NET ! (NX) 2623.05 (IT) 3323.10
<< Fleming Continental European   (IT) 2572.83
<< Gartmore European

Cash values

3600 3400 3200 3000 2800 2600 2400 2200 2000 1800 1600 1400 1200 1000 800 600

87 88 89 90 91 92 93 94 95 96

Performance Monitor 9   Source: Data Source Micropal™—© Micropal Limited 1996

Japan is a well-established large economy, and it is the health of the economy which ultimately drives an equity market. Its prowess in advancing technology puts it in the vanguard of developed country commercial success. Its business ethic is to reinvest past profits to deliver future growth and this strategy is theoretically a good one for company share prices. Japan has an efficient market. This makes a big difference because it makes the fund manager's job easier. It is easier to deal in Japanese stocks and shares, and because the market in Tokyo is well established it also maintains a supporting cast of analysts and investors.

However, investors have had fingers burnt in Japan. In 1990 the annual return from Japanese equities, expressed in sterling terms, was negative 47%. The Nikkei 225, the leading index measure of the Tokyo market, slumped from 38,000 points to 15,000 between December 1989 and June 1992.

Suitable investors

You need to be sophisticated enough to be able to draw conclusions about value for money, but a large investment portfolio of shares ought to include some exposure to the Far East. Small-scale investors can do this using a broad-based international fund, more experienced hands might do better by selecting a good performing Japan-specific fund. Again, make yourself aware of the risks as well as the rewards – see Performance Monitor 10.

Funds of the Far East including Japan

You can use the Tokyo market by itself to get a toehold into the world's most rapidly expanding exciting economic area, Asia. Countries like Korea, Taiwan, Hong Kong and China, India, Thailand, Malaysia, Singapore and Indonesia are rapidly

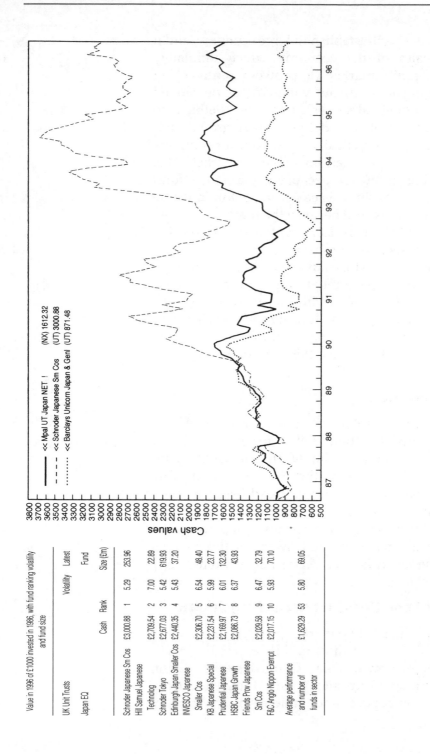

Value in 1996 of £1000 invested in 1996, with fund ranking volatility and fund size

UK Unit Trusts	Cash	Rank	Volatility	Latest Fund Size (£m)
Japan EQ				
Schroder Japanese Sm Cos	£3,000.88	1	5.29	253.96
Hill Samuel Japanese Technolog	£2,709.54	2	7.00	22.89
Schroder Tokyo	£2,677.03	3	5.42	619.93
Edinburgh Japan Smaller Cos	£2,440.35	4	5.43	37.20
INVESCO Japanese Smaller Cos	£2,306.70	5	6.54	48.40
KB Japanese Special	£2,231.54	6	5.99	23.77
Prudential Japanese	£2,169.97	7	6.01	132.30
HSBC Japan Growth	£2,086.73	8	6.37	43.93
Friends Prov Japanese Sm Cos	£2,029.58	9	6.47	32.79
F&C Anglo Nippon Exempt	£2,017.15	10	5.93	70.10
Average performance and number of funds in sector	£1,629.29	53	5.80	69.05

Legend:
— << Mpal UT Japan NET !   (NX) 1612.32
– – – << Schroder Japanese Sm Cos   (UT) 3000.88
········· << Barclays Unicorn Japan & Genl   (UT) 871.48

Cash values: 500–3800

X-axis: 87 88 89 90 91 92 93 94 95 96

Performance Monitor 10   Source: Data Source Micropal™—© Micropal Limited 1996

expanding consumer markets. Their populations are growing larger and becoming richer. Population growth is one of the primary motivating forces for economic growth, and economic growth means stock market growth.

Companies based in Japan are well placed to take advantage of these growing markets. To invest through one country's market in order to acquire exposure to another is a well-recognised stock market tactic. If you want to become more involved, think about buying a fund which invests directly into what are sometimes called the Tiger economies of the Far East. In this type of fund Japan is designed to provide the anchor role while investment elsewhere in the region provides the sparkle.

Suitable investors

The further removed you become from the established equity markets the more risk you take on. Emerging markets are notoriously volatile so while you might find yourself sitting on handsome gains one week, the next week they might disappear. Investors in the more way-out markets have to have strong constitutions. It is no use investing only to pull out at the first sign of trouble. All that does is lose you money. If you are prepared to invest for 5 or 10 years, however, you may find the volatility of these funds fades behind the performance record. Far East funds can return in 5 years what most other kinds of funds return in 10 – see Performance Monitors 11 and 12.

Funds of the Far East excluding Japan

This is an investment which is 100% exposed to the emerging markets of the Far East and is high risk. According to Micropal, unit trusts specialising in

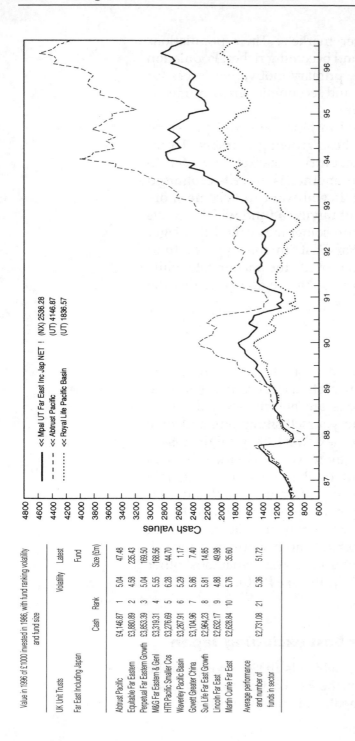

Value in 1996 of £1000 invested in 1996, with fund ranking volatility and fund size

UK Unit Trusts		Volatility	Latest
			Fund
Far East Including Japan			
	Cash	Rank	Size (£m)
Abtrust Pacific	£4,146.87	1	5.04	47.48
Equitable Far Eastern	£3,880.09	2	4.58	235.43
Perpetual Far Eastern Growth	£3,853.39	3	5.04	169.50
M&G Far Eastern & Genl	£3,319.31	4	5.55	168.56
HTR Pacific Smaller Cos	£3,276.69	5	6.28	44.70
Waverley Pacific Basin	£3,267.91	6	5.29	1.17
Govett Greater China	£3,104.96	7	5.86	7.40
Sun Life Far East Growth	£2,964.23	8	5.81	14.85
Lincoln Far East	£2,632.17	9	4.88	49.98
Martin Currie Far East	£2,628.84	10	5.76	35.60
Average performance and number of funds in sector	£2,731.08	21	5.36	51.72

Legend (on chart):
<< Mpal UT Far East Inc Jap NET ! (NX) 2536.28
<< Abtrust Pacific (UT) 4146.87
<< Royal Life Pacific Basin (UT) 1836.57

Cash values: 4800, 4600, 4400, 4200, 4000, 3800, 3600, 3400, 3200, 3000, 2800, 2600, 2400, 2200, 2000, 1800, 1600, 1400, 1200, 1000, 800, 600

X-axis: 87 88 89 90 91 92 93 94 95 96

Performance Monitor 11   Source: Data Source Micropal™—© Micropal Limited 1996

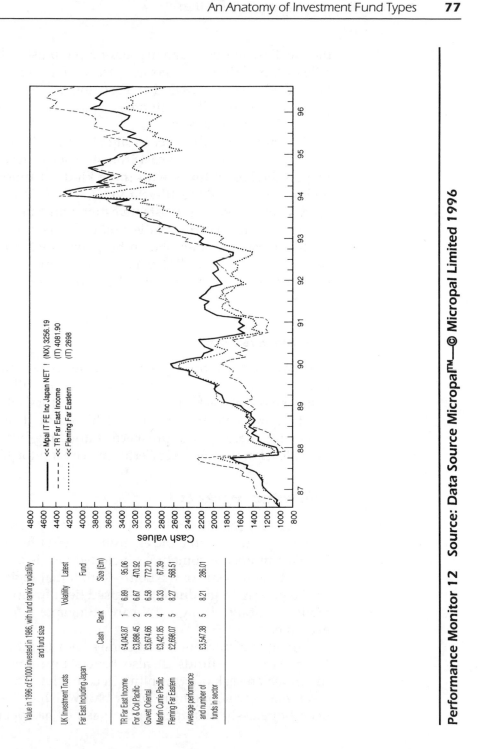

Performance Monitor 12   Source: Data Source Micropal™—© Micropal Limited 1996

the Far East minus Japan are among the most volatile group of the 25 categories it tracks. During the year to 31 October 1995, Far East unit trusts also performed abysmally, with only the top two funds out of 72 showing a profit.

But high risk also means high reward. Investors with patience—and cast iron stomachs—have reaped the best returns with these kinds of funds on both the 5- and the 10-year view. It is a similar story with investment trusts investing with similar criteria. The funds are volatile, and the scars of that unsteadiness are often shown by poor short-term performance figures. But over five or more years the returns are substantially ahead of most rival sectors.

Suitable investors

You have to have time to let an investment in this kind of market grow. It may need time to fall in value before it rises. It is also for investors who want capital growth. As with all high-growth investments there is little prospect of anything but a token level of income – see Performance Monitor 13.

Emerging markets

At the very exotic end of the investment risk–reward spectrum come the emerging market funds. Far East funds are sometimes included in this category although some of the bourses from that region are beginning to graduate to a raised tier of respectability: Hong Kong, Taiwan, Singapore, for example.

Emerging markets is sometimes shorthand for Latin American funds. It also covers investment funds which seek opportunities in countries where economic development is either backward, or has been hopelessly managed in the past, or has been otherwise constricted. In this group is South America, Eastern Europe, South Africa, China and India.

Suitable investors

Far East funds are risky but have demonstrated a track record that suggests they involve taking a risk where it is perfectly reasonable to expect a decent reward. Some of the more way-out markets cannot demonstrate such a record. It is good to remember what emerging countries (and companies) were before they emerged. They were submerged, and could resubmerge.

Emerging market funds are for the bravest of investors. Money invested here has to be viewed as risk capital, that is, money you could comfortably lose. The bravest investors are sometimes the biggest losers, but they are also among the biggest winners.

SECTION 3: SPECIALIST FUNDS

Money Market Funds

Money market funds, sometimes called cash funds, are among the least well known. Here the underlying investment is in bank deposits. They have value because by collecting large sums of money together the managers can invest at the very best rates of interest available. They also monitor competing rates, and switch funds around in order to keep the money earning the best available.

If you have small sums deposited with the bank or building society you will receive low rates of interest. As the sums of money you save grow, so does the rate of interest. With money market funds—so-called because they invest in the money markets where international banks lend and borrow

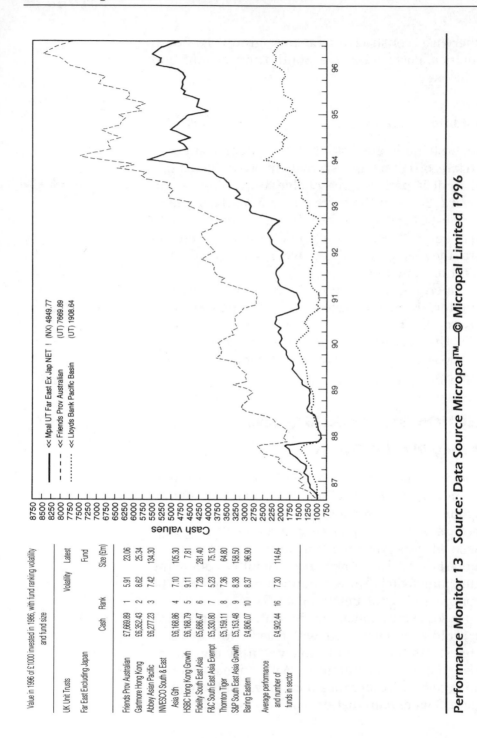

Value in 1996 of £1000 invested in 1996, with fund ranking volatility and fund size

UK Unit Trusts	Cash	Rank	Volatility	Latest Fund Size (£m)
Far East Excluding Japan				
Friends Prov Australian	£7,669.89	1	5.91	23.06
Gartmore Hong Kong	£6,352.43	2	8.62	25.34
Abbey Asian Pacific	£6,277.23	3	7.42	134.30
INVESCO South & East Asia Gth	£6,168.86	4	7.10	105.30
HSBC Hong Kong Growth	£6,168.79	5	9.11	7.81
Fidelity South East Asia	£5,686.47	6	7.28	281.40
F&C South East Asia Exempt	£5,330.80	7	5.23	75.13
Thornton Tiger	£5,159.11	8	7.36	64.80
S&P South East Asia Growth	£5,153.48	9	8.38	158.50
Baring Eastern	£4,806.07	10	8.37	96.90
Average performance and number of funds in sector	£4,902.44	16	7.30	114.64

Cash values

<< Mpal UT Far East Ex Jap NET ! (NX) 4849.77
<< Friends Prov Australian (UT) 7669.89
<< Lloyds Bank Pacific Basin (UT) 1908.64

Performance Monitor 13   Source: Data Source Micropal™—© Micropal Limited 1996

money—you can earn top rates even if you have only modest savings.

Suitable investors

People who want ease of access to money and the security of knowledge that the value of their savings is extremely unlikely to fall. Suitable investors are those who want minimum risk, but want to maximise the returns from deposits—an historically low growth investment type.

Bond Funds

Bonds are loans—usually raised either by a government or a company. A bond is usually repaid on a predetermined date and at a predetermined price, and for these reasons the scope for capital gains and losses with a bond is limited. The main attraction to investors is the level of interest a bond pays. UK government bonds are often called gilts because the bond certificates used to be edged with gold leaf, a signifier of the issuer's creditworthiness. US government bonds are called US Treasuries or T-Bills. German government bonds are known as bunds.

In buying a bond investors effectively lend money to a government or to a company. In return investors are paid interest. Issuers of bonds agree to make a series of set payments over a predefined period of time and for this reason bonds are sometimes called 'fixed interest' instruments. The fixed cash payment is sometimes called a 'coupon', because bond certificates used to have coupons attached. When each interest payment was due one coupon was torn off in exchange for the pre-agreed cash payment. If it was a 10-year bond there might be 10 coupons attached, or 20 if payments were to be made half-yearly.

Bonds—like equities—are issued in what is called the primary investment market. The primary market exists between the company or government and the investor. But bonds and shares are also freely and more commonly traded in what is termed the secondary market, which exists between investors alone.

As bonds pass between successive investors the capital value varies. As a result, and despite the fact that the actual interest payment is fixed in cash terms, the effective rate of interest also fluctuates. The effective interest rate—the so-called **yield** on a bond—changes according to the price at which a bond is traded in the months and years after it is issued and before it is redeemed.

yield: the income (perhaps via dividends) expressed as a percentage of the capital value.

Bonds are issued and redeemed in bundles of £100. This £100 is the primary market price—the issue value and the redemption value. It is also called the par value. But in the secondary market the £100 worth of bond can be bought and sold for more, or less, than the par value.

So if the annual cash payment is fixed but the value of the bond can rise and fall as it is traded it means that the yield to secondary market investors changes. If the price of the bond changes hands at a price different from par the effective interest rate—or yield—changes. For as long as £100 of bond is traded at £100 the £10 a year fixed payment is equivalent to 10% interest. But if the bond price falls to £90 the £10 a year fixed payment becomes a yield of 10 divided by 90 or 11.1%. If the bond price rises to £110 the £10 a year fixed interest payment makes the bond yield £110 divided by £10—or 9%.

The value of a bond in the secondary market depends on the fixed rate of interest it pays, and the rate of interest achievable elsewhere at a particular time. If it pays a nominal 10% a year but since issue general rates have fallen to 5% the value of the bond will increase. Similarly if general rates rise to 15% after the issue of a 10% bond its value will fall.

The mathematical mechanics are simple enough, but judging the best time to buy and sell requires expert analytical skills, a good understanding of economics and a finely tuned sense of bond market dynamics. Different bonds pay different rates of interest depending on several factors. They are:

- the general rate of interest prevailing at the time the bond is issued
- the length of term of the bond and the predicted trends in future interest rates during that term
- the quality of the creditor—financially weaker firms or governments have to pay more interest to compensate investors for taking greater risks with capital because there is more chance that weaker borrowers will welch on repayment agreements

If you are interested in gilts and fixed interest stocks you do not necessarily need to invest through a collective. You can buy them directly through a stockbroker or in the case of gilts, via the Post Office. But investors in gilt and fixed interest investment funds bypass the need to acquire the advanced analytical skills required for effective investment—they buy into the professional management offered by administrators of this type of unit or investment trust, although in pure form it is more commonly a unit trust.

Gilt and fixed interest funds used to be something of a backwater, rarely used by private investors. But the relaxation of the rules governing PEPs in 1995 to make corporate bonds eligible for inclusion has spurred private investor interest. Indeed one-third of all unit trust sales at the end of 1995 were directed at this kind of fund.

In the USA private investors are well acquainted with bond investment. Bonds are quite sensibly used as a stepping stone between low-risk saving in bank deposits and more risky equity investment. The signs are that this well-established strategy is beginning to be adopted in the UK.

Suitable investors

Bond funds are for income seekers, like pensioners. There is some room for capital growth in bond investment but it is a sideline issue. Income is what drives demand for gilts and fixed interest securities—at least among private investors – see Performance Monitor 14.

Funds of Funds

An FoF is what it says it is, an investment fund which invests the money it collects into other investment funds. Similar funds go by the name investment trust unit trusts and closed-end funds, which are investment trusts of investment trusts.

Fans of FoFs support them because are low risk. Risk is spread by the broad investment strategy followed by all funds. With FoFs the risk-spreading process operates on two levels. FoFs also have attractions because the net is spread so wide that any well-performing stock market should have an influence on the returns won by the FoF.

This is all very well, but straightforward logic also suggests that two levels of risk spreading and two levels of profit gathering also mean two levels of management charges. With an FoF you have to pay the FoF manager and the managers of each individual fund your FoF manager chooses to invest in.

Many FoFs are select investments from a range of investment funds originating from the same fund

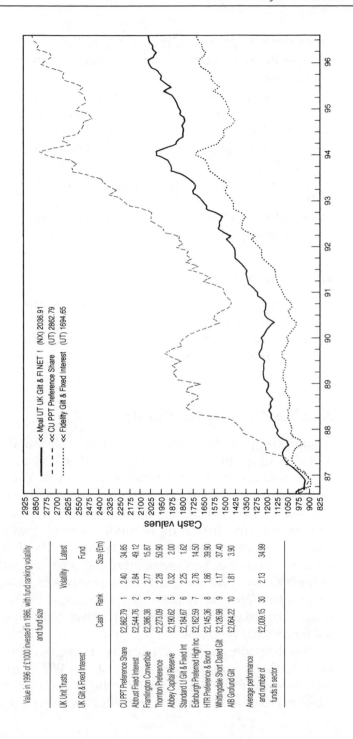

Performance Monitor 14   Source: Data Source Micropal™—© Micropal Limited 1996

management group. Other—in my view more useful—FoFs select from a wider range, selecting the best performing funds from the gamut of investment fund providers. The accusation of double charging is also countered by managers who declare that their large size and buying power mean they can buy unit trusts or investment trusts at wholesale prices. They reckon double charging is not an issue because they can bypass initial charges in the unit trusts they buy and can also negotiate preferential stockbroking commissions for the purchase of investment trusts.

Suitable investors

FoFs are another starting-point for new investors, or for more experienced investors who want some exposure to equity and bond investment funds but at very low risk, pensioners for example – see Performance Monitor 15.

Smaller Companies Funds

Smaller company investment is quite definitely at the more exciting end of the range. Smaller company investment funds invest in smaller companies. These companies are variously defined, but 'smaller' is not necessarily the same as 'small'. Smaller companies in investment fund terms are normally quoted, that is have full stock exchange accreditation. In the UK, smaller companies can mean anything which is not in the top 100, and there are 1500 or more of those companies. Of those additional 1500 quoted firms a smaller companies fund may well select only from the largest 200 or 300.

Smaller companies have several things in common with emerging markets. First, both are unproven in terms of performance, the risk of losing money is greater and the potential rewards are

Value in 1996 of £1000 invested in 1996, with fund ranking volatility and fund size

UK Unit Trusts Fund of Funds	Cash	Rank	Volatility	Latest Fund Size (£m)
Portfolio Fund of Funds	£2,011.74	1	3.31	20.51
Britannia Managed Ptfl	£1,951.52	2	3.59	123.10
Fidelity Money Builder	£1,936.85	3	3.20	179.00
Morgan Grenfell Managed	£1,800.96	4	2.65	35.39
Prudential Managed Trust	£1,794.25	5	3.31	86.10
Schroder Inst Managed Balanced	£1,782.14	6	2.78	1,360.60
Sun Alliance Portfolio	£1,701.38	7	3.37	4.00
Royal Lif Managed	£1,694.22	8	2.98	28.53
Abbey Mastertrust	£1,691.86	9	3.14	76.00
HTR Independent Portfolio	£1,658.97	10	2.97	13.10
Average performance and number of funds in sector	£1,624.87	26	3.06	66.26

<< Mpal UT Fund of Funds NET   (NX) 2234.03
<< Abbey Masterrust   (UT) 2435.17
<< Sun Life Discretionary Ptfl   (UT) 2112.27

Cash values

Performance Monitor 15   Source: Data Source Micropal™—© Micropal Limited 1996

larger as well. Smaller company investment also requires a higher level of specialist investment management expertise. In many ways it is for exactly these reasons that investment funds were invented —to spread risk and to pool resources to buy investment management expertise.

Suitable investors

Savers hungry for capital growth and who have a well developed sense of the relationship between risk and reward. Those who believe smaller companies have the potential to grow at a faster pace than their larger brethren, and be able to survive the competitive pressures larger firms are able to exert. Income via dividends from smaller companies is usually poor – see Performance Monitors 16 and 17.

Venture and Development Capital Funds

One step beyond smaller companies are unquoted companies. These funds buy shares in companies which are not traded in public market-places, like stock exchanges. Venture and development capital funds invest in start-up businesses, or management buy-outs. They may also invest in new industries or help in the development of companies exploring new technologies. Because these firms tend to have untested track records, and because young firms tend to be those that fail in largest numbers, venture and development capital funds are definitely at the risky end of the investment spectrum. Potential rewards, on the other hand, are large as well.

Note: A subsection of these funds are so-called venture capital trusts (VCTs). These attract particular tax benefits as long as the fund operates within rules set by the government. Income from VCT investment does not incur income tax; you can invest

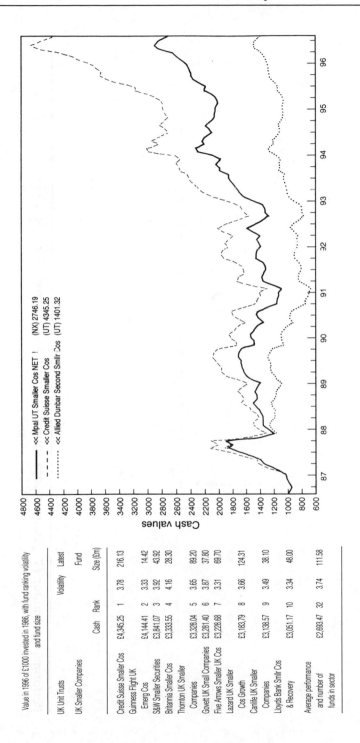

Value in 1996 of £1000 invested in 1996, with fund ranking volatility and fund size

UK Unit Trusts	Volatility		Latest
UK Smaller Companies			Fund
	Cash	Rank	Size (£m)
Credit Suisse Smaller Cos	£4,345.25	1	216.13
Guinness Flight UK			
Emerg Cos	£4,144.41	2	14.42
S&W Smaller Securities	£3,841.07	3	43.92
Britannia Smaller Cos	£3,333.55	4	28.30
Thornton UK Smaller			
Companies	£3,328.04	5	89.20
Govett UK Small Companies	£3,281.40	6	37.80
Five Arrows Smaller UK Cos	£3,228.68	7	69.70
Lazard UK Smaller			
Cos Growth	£3,183.79	8	124.31
Carlile UK Smaller			
Companies	£3,138.57	9	38.10
Lloyds Bank Smllr Cos			
& Recovery	£3,051.17	10	48.00
Average performance			
and number of	£2,693.47	32	111.58
funds in sector			

Legend:
—— << Mpal UT Smaller Cos NET !   (NX) 2746.19
– – – << Credit Suisse Smaller Cos   (UT) 4345.25
········· << Allied Dunbar Second Smllr Cos (UT) 1401.32

Cash values: 600, 800, 1000, 1200, 1400, 1600, 1800, 2000, 2200, 2400, 2600, 2800, 3000, 3200, 3400, 3600, 3800, 4000, 4200, 4400, 4600, 4800

X-axis: 87 88 89 90 91 92 93 94 95 96

Performance Monitor 16   Source: Data Source Micropal™—© Micropal Limited 1996

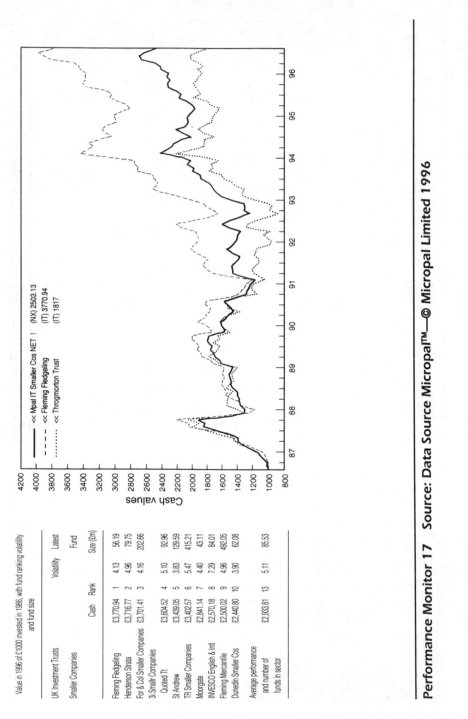

Value in 1996 of £1000 invested in 1986, with fund ranking volatility and fund size

UK Investment Trusts	Cash	Rank	Volatility	Latest Fund Size (£m)
Smaller Companies				
Fleming Fledgeling	£3,770.94	1	4.13	56.19
Henderson Strata	£3,716.77	2	4.96	79.75
For & Col Smaller Companies	£3,701.41	3	4.16	202.66
3i Smaller Companies				
Quoted Tt	£3,604.52	4	5.10	92.96
St Andrew	£3,439.05	5	3.83	129.59
TR Smaller Companies	£3,402.57	6	5.47	415.21
Moorgate	£2,841.14	7	4.40	43.11
INVESCO English & Intl	£2,570.18	8	7.29	84.01
Fleming Mercantile	£2,500.02	9	4.96	492.05
Dunedin Smaller Cos	£2,440.80	10	3.90	62.08
Average performance and number of funds in sector	£2,933.81	13	5.11	85.53

Performance Monitor 17   Source: Data Source Micropal™—© Micropal Limited 1996

up to £100,000 with up-front tax relief of 20%—which effectively means you invest £120,000 at a cost of £100,000 and capital gains tax (CGT) is not levied on the rise in the value of VCT shares. You can also roll over CGT on money released from other investments to subscribe to a VCT. CGT is payable in the end, but only when you liquidate the VCT by which time the inflation mechanism applied to CGT charges may have reduced the bill.

Rich investors may be attracted to the tax relief on VCT but they should be aware that no tactic to delay, or reduce, payment of tax is worth anything if the investment fails. Extra careful selection of a venture capital trust fund manager is required.

Suitable investors

Investors who have time to allow the value of their money to mature might be attracted to unquoted investments. If you are keen to see your money help young companies which are pushing back the frontiers of technology you may also find excitement in this arena – see Performance Monitor 18.

Country Funds

Country funds invest in particular in the shares of companies based in one particular foreign state. A pedant could call UK, US or Japanese funds country funds. However, common usage is to call funds which specialise in one second- or third-tier stock market a country fund. Many country funds are German or French, but several others exist as well. There is a small handful of funds which invest in Australian companies, New Zealand firms, or a combination.

It became very fashionable to launch India funds in 1995 and 1996. China-specific funds have

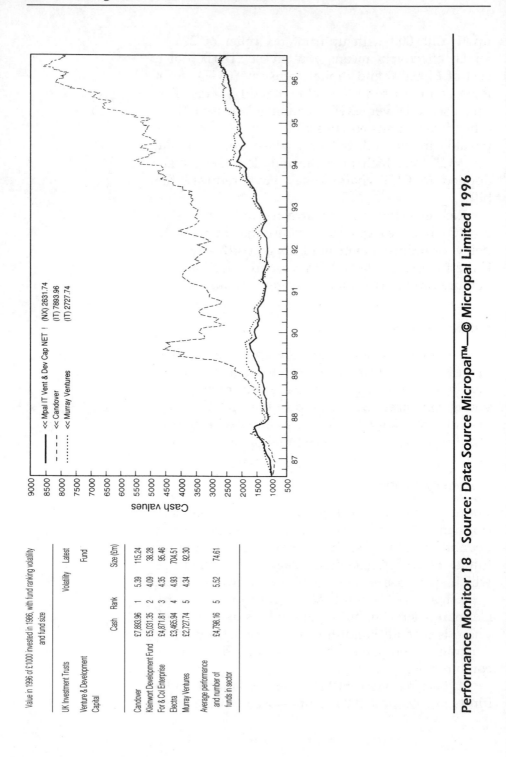

UK Investment Trusts		Volatility	Latest	
			Fund	
Venture & Development				
Capital				
	Cash	Rank		Size (£m)
Candover	£7,893.96	1	5.39	115.24
Kleinwort Development Fund	£5,031.35	2	4.09	38.28
For & Col Enterprise	£4,871.81	3	4.35	95.46
Electra	£3,465.94	4	4.93	704.51
Murray Ventures	£2,727.74	5	4.34	92.30
Average performance				
and number of	£4,798.16	5	5.52	74.61
funds in sector				

Value in 1996 of £1000 invested in 1986, with fund ranking volatility and fund size

Legend: << Mpal IT Vent & Dev Cap NET ! (NX) 2631.74 (IT) 7893.96; << Candover; << Murray Ventures (IT) 2727.74

Cash values

Performance Monitor 18   **Source: Data Source Micropal™—© Micropal Limited 1996**

also appeared along with ones for South Africa, Chile, Israel, Hungary and the silliest named trust of them all, the Turkey Trust.

Suitable investors

As a general rule the more specialist the fund, the less interest there is for private investors and the more it is designed to cater for professional fund managers who want some exposure to these niche areas for, perhaps, a multimillion pound pension fund portfolio.

However, if you fancy a particular investment idea there is no reason why individuals should not buy in as well. It is worth suggesting, however, that very specialist funds ought to constitute a minority part of a portfolio of investments.

Sector Funds

Sector funds are similar to country funds except that the investment remit is narrowly defined. Sector funds are defined by the type of business that is transacted by the companies whose shares are owned by the fund, or by the kind of assets owned by the fund. Therefore there are property funds, either which invest in property company shares or which invest directly in property. Property funds which invest directly into bricks and mortar traditionally bought commercial or industrial property but in the Budget of 1995 the government allowed investment directly into residential property too— ostensibly to increase the availability of private rented housing. These are termed housing investment trusts.

Similarly there are energy funds, sometimes called oil and gas funds, which invest in the shares of companies which extract, transport or sell oil and gas. Some of these funds invest directly into projects which explore for and develop oil and gas fields. The same story goes for mineral extraction.

There are funds which specialise in financial companies, investing into banks and life insurance companies. Also there are commodities funds which buy and sell commodities like gold or copper.

Suitable investors

Again, suitable investors are those with a narrowly defined ambition or need which coincides with the aims and objectives of the fund.

Other Funds

There is also a long tail of miscellaneous funds which operate to serve particular purposes. Investment fund managers are continually dreaming up new themes on which to base funds.

Funds have been launched to invest specifically in European privatisation issues. There are several funds which buy second-hand endowment policies—the long-term stock market linked savings schemes. Individuals were sold these long-term life insurance linked investments by the million in the 1980s. Many were attached to home loans but the long term nature of the savings contract—especially the ones designed to be fed by monthly premiums—proved to be unsuitable for some consumers. So many wanted to get rid of unwanted endowments that a second-hand market grew up. Impatience, unexpected poverty, and marital break-up were the main reasons why people wanted to stop contributing to what have been rewarding, but inflexible, stock market savings vehicles.

Second-hand buyers, some of whom were investment funds, were prepared to pay better prices than were achievable by surrendering the policies back to the insurance company issuer. They paid better prices because they could see and were prepared to be patient enough to wait for the long-term returns that stock market investments provide.

Funds have been set up which attract capital for investment in the Lloyd's of London insurance market. Funds exist which invest in warrants of companies or of investment trusts, also in split capital investment trusts—and normally specialise in dealing with either the capital portion of the split or the income part.

Other funds exist which buy derivatives. Derivatives is a term which has earned itself a bad reputation following the disastrously injudicious use of the instruments by Nick Leeson of Barings. However derivatives, sometimes called 'futures and options', can be a very useful weapon for managing volatility and risk, rather than exposing oneself to it. A whole book could be written on the use of derivatives, but in simple form ownership of a derivative does not mean you own an asset but only the right to buy or sell that asset to a third party at some time in the future.

Futures and options funds are normally the preserve of institutional investors. There are also legions of different derivatives contracts struck between buyers and sellers with quite specific objectives. It is hard to simplify because derivative products vary, and the needs of buyers and sellers of the instrument are, superficially at least, hard to reconcile. However, one simple example of how risk can be reduced using derivatives is this: say you own shares in BP at 500p a share. You may believe they are going to rise in value, so buy some more. But just in case they do not rise in value you may also buy an option to sell those shares to a third party in one year at 500p. You pay for that option, but the option price is a fraction of the price of the shares themselves. If the price of BP shares unexpectedly falls to 300p you have insulated yourself from much of the loss because you have the right to sell at 500p.

Warrants, as described in Chapter 3, are a form of option and there are funds which specialise in investing in these instruments.

Suitable investors

The same investor profile for sector funds and country funds applies here. Specialist funds satisfy specialist needs.

POSTSCRIPT ON GUARANTEED FUNDS

In the last year or two a newish breed of investment fund has grown up, called the guaranteed fund or protected fund. These are not usually either investment trusts or unit trusts but the popularity of the genre means it would not be sensible for me to leave them out of this survey.

First be careful of the name. Guarantees are extremely attractive to investors and the term can be bandied about by promoters of funds in order to give a sense of security that may not be justified. Remember the verity: a guarantee is only as secure as the guarantor. Protected or secure funds are other more sober names for this kind of fund.

Typical guaranteed, protected or secure funds work like this. At the outset a promise is made that in, say, five years' time you will receive growth in your investment related to the growth in a stock market index, commonly the FTSE 100. But you are also promised that if the stock market falls over that period you will get your money back in full. Sometimes the minimum guaranteed return is greater than the original investment.

Over and above the minimum, returns are only 'related' to the growth in the index. You rarely get full growth, that is you rarely get a 50% return if the index grows by 50%. You may be promised a proportion of the returns, say 60% of the growth. In translation this means you would get 60% of 50%. Which is 30%. There may also be a ceiling imposed so that you get no more than, say, a 75% return even if the relevant index grows in such a way that the formula ought to return more than this.

So how do the guarantees operate? Your investment is split into two parts. The larger portion is put on deposit at a bank at a fixed rate of interest. The exact amount will vary, but the idea is that this sum will grow to be equal to the minimum guaranteed repayment promised by the fund manager. The rest of your investment—usually a smaller portion of the whole—is used to secure the stock market growth element. This is done using options. An option holder has the right to buy or sell an asset at a predetermined date in the future at a predetermined price. The manager of a guaranteed fund may invest in an option to buy assets which reflect the value of the index at today's price five years hence. If the actual value rises in five years the manager can exercise the right to buy at the old price, then immediately sell at the new price. The profit is the difference between the two, minus the original cost of the option. This profit provides the stock market linkage.

If the value of the index falls the fund manager can choose not to exercise the option to buy, in which case the cost of the exercise is limited to the original cost of buying the option. But since that cost was covered by the interest earned on the deposited money the minimum guaranteed return is not affected.

By way of illustration, consider this example. Say you invested £1000 in one of these funds and agreed to keep the investment for five years. The fund manager may put £900 of the £1000 on deposit at a fixed interest rate of 6%. In five years this will turn £900 into £1200 and thus provide the guarantee.

With the other £100 of the £1000 options are bought. The cost of an option varies according to the precise situation, but is less than the cost of the actual asset over which the option is held. Say the index measure is at 2000 at the start of the investment period, and that is the level at which the manager secures the right to buy five years down the line. Let us then say that the index rises by 50% to 3000. We can then assume that the manager, exercising his option to buy, pays £1000 for an asset worth £1500 making a profit of £500.

The total profit to the manager is £1700 (£1200 from the deposited money + £500 from the option) or 70% (£1000 to £1700). The manager wants a cut so in accordance with an agreement made at the outset hands you on only part of the profit, say 60%. But remember you only get a porportion of the growth in the index measure, not the overall growth of the investment. So you get 60% of a 50% rise—or 30%. In other words, the overall investment grows from £1000 to £1700 but your return is only £1300 from £1000.

Each individual 'guaranteed', 'protected' or 'secure' fund will be slightly different but usually works according to a formula similar to that outlined above. Assuming you buy from a reputable firm there is nothing wrong with them, but you should be aware of the cost of securing the guarantee. You may not get the full amount of growth managed by an index, and the index growth measure used rarely includes dividend income reinvestment. The reinvestment of dividend income makes an enormous difference, but is easily forgotten about by private investors and glossed over by the promoters of such products. Over five years the reinvestment of dividend income can be double the capital-value-only returns from a stock market investment.

Guaranteed funds are all very well for the cautious investor and can bring returns slightly better than from deposits. If you are happy to restrict your upside for the peace of mind a guaranteed product brings, they are fine. But the cost to the upside should not be underestimated.

What a Performance: Making the Most of Saving with Investment Funds

There is a well-known retailing adage which states that the three vital things to consider when opening a shop are location, location and location. This saying is easily adapted to making a decision about investing in collectives. It is about performance, performance and performance.

This chapter shows investors how to find out about and analyse past performance, and make estimations about future performance. It stresses the importance of adopting realistic expectations.

It also covers reading performance tables printed in newspapers and how to see through potentially misleading statistical jiggery-pokery.

PERFORMANCE IS PARAMOUNT

Performance is what it is all about. Performance is the acid test. Performance is what every investor is after and what every fund manager wants to deliver.

Performance distinguishes one fund manager from another. Choosing a fund manager is largely about making judgements about the potential a fund manager has for delivering performance. Monitoring investments is largely about measuring the performance of a fund manager against several benchmarks and deciding whether you would be better off changing the manager you have selected to look after your money.

It sounds simple enough. Unfortunately, however, assessing the potential for performance delivery is not only the most important aspect of investment it is also the most difficult. It is difficult for three reasons. Firstly, doubt. Although history tells us that it is highly likely that stock markets will deliver good, inflation-beating, returns there is no absolute certainty. In theory, the whole system could collapse. Revolution and war have destroyed capitalist systems in the past, and could do so again. More likely is that individual funds could fall apart through mismanagement or fraud.

Put the prospect of calamity in context, however. The chances of complete failure are tiny when compared to the likelihood that if you do not save you may end up poor. The disaster risk is also small when compared to the probability that if you do not invest in equities the value of your money will be seriously eroded by inflation.

Secondly, assessing performance is difficult because performance statistics themselves can be massaged. Do the past performance statistics you are examining include the effect of fees and charges? Do they encompass capital growth only? Is any income derived from the investment in shares reinvested, distributed or siphoned off by the manager? Is anything being hidden by the time period over which past performance is being assessed?

Thirdly, the mechanics of obtaining performance statistics is not easy. Learning how to read them once you do get hold of them is a skill in itself.

PAST PERFORMANCE

As every investment advertisement is obliged to state, past performance is no guarantee of future success, only an indication of what may come about assuming that past experience is replicated in future.

In the land of the blind, however, the one-eyed man is king. Past performance is one of the best clues we have about future returns. It may sound silly to say it of the world of finance, a world that by reputation is hard-bitten and cynical, but its continuing survival does depend on an element of faith. To get involved you have to assume that in broad terms what has gone before will be repeated in the future.

Figures 6.1 and 6.2 present an excellent overview of past performance. They plot the number of successive 5- and 10-year periods during which the FTSE All Share index performance can be categorised into the segments shown. It is because each 5- and 10-year period starts and ends on a different day that makes the graph so useful and informative. The private investor's start date, after all, may be selected more or less at random—perhaps depending when a legacy is received or when a pension fund matures. The graphs give an idea of the chances of success given a random start date selection. Judging by past performance there is a 75% chance that the FTSE All Share index, with dividend income reinvested, will increase in value by more than 50% over five years. There is a 6% chance it will fall in value. Over successive 10-year periods there is 86% chance that the index will double and just a 1% chance it will fall in value.

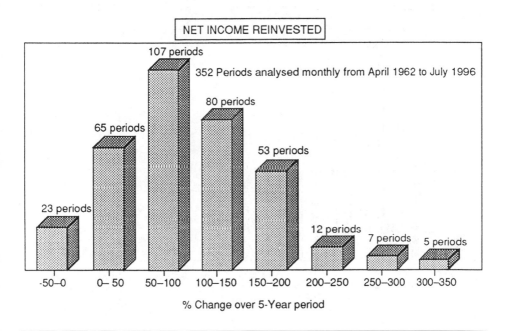

Figure 6.1   FTSE All Share Index performance in successive five-year roll-ing periods. Source: M&G

These graphs may be difficult to read at first but it is worth persevering until you understand what they show because they provide some of the best evidence to counter the widely held view that stock market investment is inherently and commonly risky.

But there are two important riders to add to the evidence provided by the graphs. The performance of the FTSE All Share index may not mirror the performance of a particular investment fund you select. The FTSE All Share index, with dividend income reinvested, is a demanding benchmark to match not least because no account is taken of inevitable costs and charges that come with investment funds.

The second rider is that the statistics have been drawn from a relatively short period and do not

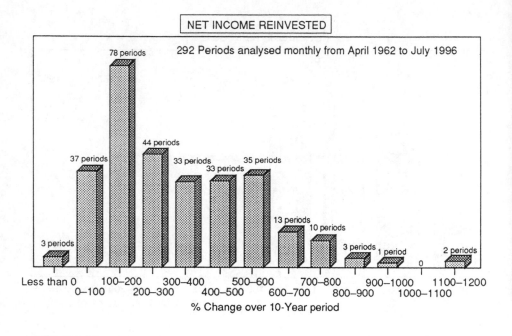

Figure 6.2   FTSE All Share Index performance in successive 10-year rolling periods. Source: M&G

include figures from the least successful periods of stock market investment. In the early 1920s, during the depression of the 1930s, post-Second World War and during the oil crisis of 1973–1975, equity investment and to some extent bond investment were poor. Investors over 5 and 10 years in average or even above average performing funds during these periods could well have been disappointed. If we hit another crisis period like the ones that have gone before, much of the currently justifiable optimism and confidence could evaporate. The lessons from the disastrous performance of the Tokyo market in the early part of the 1990s should also be learnt.

But before you get too worried about the prospect of a deep and long-lasting bear market consider what was happening on the world stage, and in economics, during these past periods of investment despair. In the 1920s and late 1940s and early 1950s the economy and the stock markets were ravaged by the after-effects of world war. In the 1930s economic depression cast an enormous cloud. And in 1973–1975 there was a large hike in the cost of the world's most important raw material and energy source, oil. The more recent Japan experience may be explained away by pointing to peculiar economic and political upheavals as an overheated emerging market emerged into the First World and suffered its first substantial economic setback.

So before getting too concerned about another prolonged bear market ask yourself whether these sorts of world-shaking events are likely to intrude on the investment scene.

TOTAL RETURN

Be clear about your performance measures. Professionals calculate total return, and it is the only really useful measure of whether an investment has succeeded or failed.

It is especially important to be aware of **total return** with high income funds which allow themselves to dig into capital to honour a predetermined promise to pay a certain level of income. Income may be constant at, say, 6% a year but if the capital value of the fund declines by 2% in order to pay that income the total return for that year is 4%.

Do not be tempted to ignore one-offs. Unpleasant surprises are part and parcel of all investment. It is funny how easy it is to regard an unexpected setback as an ignorable one-off, which should not be allowed to spoil an otherwise sound underlying performance. It is usually equally easy, however, to convince yourself that a windfall profit is the result of an inspired investment decision, the results of

total return: the most important figure. It is total profits when all levies and charges have been accounted for. May be calculated on an annualised basis.

which it is only fair to include in the overall performance picture. All gains and losses should be taken into account. Do not be tempted to ignore the effect of dealing costs or tax, for example. These impact on the success or otherwise of an investment and should therefore be factored into the equation.

Be careful to include all the plus points too. In particular, do not forget to include the returns from dividend income as well as capital growth. It is all too easy to check back and find out what you paid for a fund, subtract that from its current value, and be tempted to call that your loss or gain. But a true picture includes any dividends or income that may have been paid during the period.

EVERYTHING IS RELATIVE

You need to get a firm grip on the relative nature of investment performance in order to adopt realistic expectations about returns. There is only one constant in the world of investment, and that is that everything is constantly changing. Failure to appreciate this salience is probably the root cause of widespread and alarming ignorance about finance, business and economics.

Quite understandably, people want certainty. People want anchor points from which they can gauge what is going on. Unfortunately, no such unequivocal and unambiguous invariants exist. It is probably because there are no certainties that people quickly feel drowned in the complexities of investment. In fact, while the waters of finance can move fast, be turbulent and swirl in strange patterns, the water is also quite shallow.

None the less most things in finance only have relevance in relation to other things precisely because all things are in perpetual motion. A company's annual profit only really says anything about a company's fortunes when it is compared with the previous year—or perhaps a forecast of next year's likely out-turn. What does it mean to have secured pre-tax profits of £100 million? Very little, unless you relate the figure. If the company made £50 million last time you get an indication that a company is doing well. If it made £200 million previously, you can draw more negative conclusions.

The same principle is true when approaching and assessing investment funds. Here, however, the rate of inflation is probably the most important point of comparison. Prices have been rising at varying rates since the start of time, and in order to maintain standards of living it is necessary to keep up with inflation. Inflation is every saver's worst enemy because it erodes the value of money. Outpacing inflation is one of the most worthwhile aims of investment.

If you have difficulty grasping this concept consider that the average salary in 1971 was £1600 a year compared to £17,500 in 1996. Then ask yourself how you would like to survive on £1600 a year now because if you had made no attempt to protect yourself from inflation you would have to. Figure 6.3 shows how much prices have risen since 1971.

Apart from inflation you should set your objectives and judge the performance of your investments against other measures. Interest rates represent a key benchmark. For many professional investors base rates define a minimum level of investment return. Any fool can put money in the bank and earn money in a virtually risk-free environment. The hassle and the risk of equity investment are only worth it if you are going to do better than what any fool can manage.

For investors in investment funds the returns achievable by saving at bank base rate can usefully be seen as zero, the neutral position. If you earn less than bank base rate you are paying a price: if you earn more you are ahead of the game. It is for this reason that building societies are so patronised

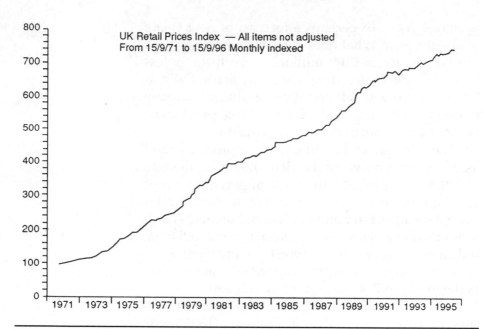

Figure 6.3   Retail price index since 1971. Source: Datastream. Reproduced by permission of Datastream International

and ridiculed by professional investors. Rarely can you earn the equivalent of bank base rate with a building society. There is commonly a difference of at least two percentage points. Therefore in some senses you actually endure a negative return sticking to the building society.

But then again because it is quite difficult for the small investor to get access to bank base interest rate returns it might be more relevant to use the interest on a building society account as your interest rate benchmark, perhaps one of the high interest rate accounts. It depends on your standpoint, which is itself another thing that makes everything else relative.

BENCHMARKS

Equity investment, over the long term, should produce better returns than interest rates. But as you increase your expectations of rewards, so you expose yourself to greater levels of risk.

Once you are convinced by the attraction of equities, however, a good benchmark is the FTSE 100 index of Britain's largest quoted companies. Alternatively you might look at the FTSE All Share index, a more comprehensive measure of market performance because its data base includes more stocks: it tracks about 900 companies (about half the total number) whose share price is quoted on the London Stock Exchange. You may look at the performance of a more specialised industrial sector average, for example utility companies or leisure sector firms. You might monitor an overseas index like the Dow Jones Industrial Average of US stocks—although the Standard & Poors' Index of 500 is a better, more thorough, yardstick.

There are hundreds of different measures which you could look at, but most people are constricted because they do not have access to the information services that professional investors can easily look at. Private investors usually have to settle for the information selected and presented by financial journals. They usually go for the well-known indices like those mentioned above, together with others like the Japanese Nikkei 225, or the Hang-Seng Index from Hong Kong. The *Financial Times (FT)*, on a Saturday, makes a good effort to provide a good spread of benchmarking information.

These benchmarks discussed so far are actual measures. More sophisticated investors want to gauge progression after making allowances for inflation. Inflation-adjusted returns are commonly referred to as 'real' returns. (Pedants might say that inflation-adjusted returns are quite the opposite from real, but in this sense real does not mean actual. Real values are values adjusted for increasing prices.)

It is because the rate of inflation is the king benchmark that professional investors adjust most other yardsticks to take account of it. One of the most authoritative and best respected assessments of investment returns is the annual 'Gilt–Equity Study' from the stockbroker Barclays de Zoete Wedd (BZW). Some of its measures are adjusted for inflation, because it is what professional investors expect. For private investors, the professionals provide a good lead to follow on this one. A direct quote from BZW's most recent Gilt–Equity Study, published in January 1996, explains the value of inflation-adjusted benchmarks:

> The BZW indices record the total returns produced at annual intervals since December 1918. A £100 invested in the UK equity market then and allowing for the reinvestment of gross dividends would have been valued at £617,057 at the end of December 1995. The equivalent figure for gilts would be £8,279 . . . Allowance should be made for inflation, and this would reduce the figures to £32,612 for equities, £438 for gilts . . . This still represents a considerable out performance by equities.
>
> If the same calculations are performed for the post second war period alone, £100 invested in December 1945 would now be worth £51,373 if invested in equities and £1,945 for gilts . . . Again allowing for inflation the respective figures are £2,505 for equities and £95 for gilts.

Perhaps most tellingly for private investors the 1996 report continues:

> We have provided a comparison using building society ordinary deposit rates net of the basic rate of income tax since 1946. To provide a direct comparison with equities we have calculated the progress of an equity investment of £100 in December 1945 with dividends reinvested net of the basic rate of income tax. At the end of December 1995 the

equity fund would have been worth £21,814. The equivalent building society fund would have risen to £1,040. Allowing for inflation the figures are £1,064 and £51 respectively. The real value of an investment in cash would therefore have halved over a 50 year period while an equity portfolio would have increased tenfold.

The annual updated document is also respected because it summarises different kinds of investment return over a very long period of time. By stretching back to 1918 the survey provides an invaluable historical overview: and while past performance provides no guarantee of future prospects it is one of the best guides we have.

To my mind, inflation-adjusted performance statistics like the ones listed in the BZW quotation, make the most forceful case there is for investment fund investment. This lesson is illustrated in Figures 6.4 and 6.5. The graphs show that since 1945 equities have done 20–25 times better than building society deposits. Figure 6.4 shows that money invested in a building society has actually halved in value when inflation is taken into account. It is only fair to note that most of the damage to the real value of money held in a building society since 1945 was done in the high inflation period of the 1970s. Before, and since, you may have been able to keep ahead of inflation with the bank and building society assuming you got access to best rates. The stumbling block for many small investors, however, is that you may not be able to get at bank or building society best interest rates. You need to deposit large sums with banks or building societies to benefit from inflation-beating interest rates. No such huge sums are needed to access the inflation-beating investment funds. In any event the investment fund returns are, on the whole, far better anyway.

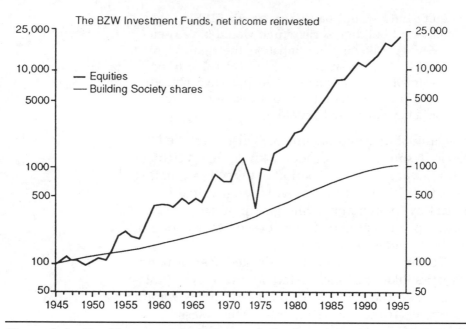

The BZW Investment Funds, net income reinvested

— Equities
— Building Society shares

Figure 6.4 Equities versus building societies log scale. Source: Exhibit 56 from BZW Equity–Gilt Study, January 1996. Reproduced by permission of Barclays de Zoete Wedd

ASSESSING INDIVIDUAL FUND PERFORMANCE

It is quite easy to gain confidence in the future of investment by looking at average performance records of all unit trusts, all investment trusts, or of index measures. But these are theoretical measures. How do you go about assessing a particular investment fund's performance and compare it to others that may attract you?

The answer is that you have to examine past performance statistics. The exercise takes some dedication and many may find it dull, but if you are serious about investment it has to be done because it is only by surveying and monitoring past performance statistics that you can hope to make good investment judgements.

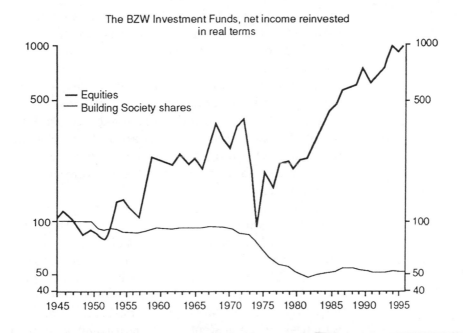

Figure 6.5   Equities versus building societies adjusted for inflation log scale. Source: Exhibit 57 from BZW Equity–Gilt Study, January 1996. Reproduced by permission of Barclays de Zoete Wedd

Once you have familiarised yourself with the way figures are presented the information is not all that tricky to find. One of the most comprehensive and easily accessible sources is in *Money Management* magazine.

In *Money Management* performance tables list figures for unit trusts and investment trusts separately. As I have said elsewhere in this book, investment trusts and unit trusts share much in common, particularly from a private investor's point of view. However, the prices of each are published separately because the price of units in a unit trust and shares in an investment trust company are calculated in different ways. Most notably with an investment trust company there is the difference between net asset value and actual share price.

Money Management also publishes performance statistics for insurance funds and offshore funds, so first find the relevant sections on unit and investment trusts.

Past performance statistics in *Money Management* are made easier to read because they show the value of £1000 invested. This makes comparison much simpler because it gets around the obstruction that each fund, each unit and each investment trust share have a different—not comparable—actual price.

Money Management splits unit trusts and investment trusts into sectors. Sector by sector each fund is listed, and performance figures given over several time periods. The number represents the current value of £1000 had it been invested 1 month ago, 6 months ago, 1 year ago, 2 years ago, 3 years ago, 5 years ago and 10 years ago. The best funds are those which show consistent good performance over all or most of the time periods. Performance over long time periods is more telling than over shorter ones because it points to greater reliability.

annualised growth rate: total returns over a number of years averaged out to give an annual figure.

Another figure in *Money Management* which measures consistency is the AGR—the **annualised growth rate**. These are given over 5 and 10 years. In simple terms a 5-year AGR is the total return over 5 years divided by 5.

Building up expertise in fund performance is like putting a jigsaw together. But do not expect to finish the puzzle completely. The best you can do is get a good impression. In the search for perfection there will always be some pieces missing. And even if you could finish the puzzle it would only give you a picture of past performance—the future may be different.

If you spend your time looking for the best performer, and you set yourself expectations to choose the best performer every time, you will wear yourself out, become frustrated, and probably ultimately fail. It is better to widen the measure of success by attempting to select funds which consistently appear in the top 25%. These are called top quartile funds. In *Money Management* each individual fund is assigned a performance ranking, sector by sector. The number of funds in each sector is also given at the bottom of the list so it is not hard to calculate which come in the top 25%. *Money Management* makes the job easier by highlighting top quartile funds in bold type.

After reading Chapter 5 you may have some idea of what kind of fund you are interested in. Much of this decision will be based on how much risk you are prepared to take in search of reward. It will be best to compare performance of similarly constituted unit trust funds with investment trust funds and vice versa. You should also cross-refer with other types of fund and with more general benchmark indicators (inflation rates, returns from building society deposits, stock market index measures and average performance numbers for unit and investment trusts). These are tabulated by *Money Management* at the beginning of its statistics section.

As well as performance statistics *Money Management* gives other very useful pieces of information. It shows how large a fund is in terms of pounds invested. Working on the principle that there is safety in numbers you might like to show preference for bigger funds. Also the best fund managers will gravitate towards the bigger funds because that is where their influence will be greatest and talent shown off to best effect. Bigger funds also earn bigger fees (in money rather than percentage of fund value terms) and may pay the largest salaries.

Money Management also shows when each fund was launched, and you can draw some comfort that the older established funds are more tried and tested. *Money Management* also shows a volatility rating upwards from 0. Low figures indicate low volatility, which in turn suggests lower-risk funds.

Assessing particular funds is a question of synthesising all the evidence. No one figure will put one fund above another, but if you take all the evidence together you can sort the wheat from the chaff.

MONITORING INDIVIDUAL FUND PERFORMANCE

If you own either investment trusts or unit trusts already you can look up prices of trusts in most quality broadsheet papers. The *FT* provides the most comprehensive service.

Unit Trusts

If it is a unit trust you are after look up the unit trust section. In the *FT* unit trust funds are categorised alphabetically according to fund management group, then the individual funds run by each group are listed under the heading of the management group. If, for example, you are looking for the Income Unit Trust from fund manager Jupiter first look for Jupiter, then the Income Fund which will be in a subsection under the Jupiter name.

In the *FT* there are several pages dedicated to the price of funds, in pages headed 'FT Managed Funds Service'. Some of the funds are based off shore in various different locations around the world, some are insurance funds. This book deals with funds registered in the UK only (although much of what pertains to onshore funds also applies to offshore funds, and insurance funds for that matter). However, make sure you go to the right section, and for the most commonly held unit trusts, in the *FT*, this is under the title 'Authorised Unit Trusts'.

There are several figures beside the name of each fund. For getting a price, however, two are important. These are often called the 'offer' price and the 'bid' price but helpfully the *FT* uses less jargon, calling the two the 'selling price' and the 'buying price' respectively. However, it still takes some hard concentration to work out which is which. It is confusing mostly because for every trade there is a buyer and a seller, so one man's buying price is another's selling price, and vice versa. The investor buying price is called the offer price because that is the price at which units or shares are offered for sale by the fund manager. The investor selling price is called the bid price because that is the price at which the fund manager will bid, auction-like, for your units.

The easiest way to cut through the terminology is to remember that as a private investor you will always pay the higher price when you buy, and always get the lower price when you sell.

If you want to know the value of an investment you already own, you should look at the bid price, the lower price, because this is what you would get if you sold. If you want to know how an investment has performed you need to multiply the bid price by the number of units you own and subtract from this total the sum of your original investment.

Having two prices depending on whether you are a buyer or a seller is undoubtedly confusing, and it would be much simpler if there was just one price. But the margin in between is what is left to the middleman—in this case the fund management group, who may share some of this cash with a financial adviser or broker. It is annoying to pay the middleman but if there was no cash for the middleman he or she or it would not exist. If the middleman was not there there would be no public market and you would not be able to buy or sell the shares as easily as you can under the present system.

The margin or—spread—does vary from fund management group to fund management group. Different types of fund also tend to have spreads calculated according to different scales. It can be as much as 10% of the value of the unit or as little as a fraction of a per cent. Usually it is of the order of 5–6%. With unit trusts, the size of the spread is inextricably tied up with the charges made by the fund manager, and I will return to this issue in Chapter 8.

For the moment, when it comes to assessing fund performance remember two things. First, that prices are easily accessible through the *FT* and other papers, and second that you calculate the value of your investment by using the lower of the two prices quoted.

Investment Trusts

For investment trusts the prices are grouped together on the share price pages showing the share prices for all quoted companies. You need to look for the sub-section dedicated to investment trusts and within the sector investment trusts are listed alphabetically by name of trust, rather than by fund management group, although names of funds are often prefixed with the name of a fund management group.

bid offer spread: the difference between the price at which an investor buys and the price at which he sells an investment.

As for unit trusts there is an offer (investor buying) price and a bid (investor selling) price for investment trust shares. In fact there is a **bid to offer spread** on all share price quotations. However, when it comes to investment trust shares and other trading company shares most publications—including the *FT*—print one price only. This is called a mid market price and as the title suggests is half-way between the offer and bid prices.

Mid market price information is usually sufficient because the spreads on investment trust shares are very small, usually a fraction of a per cent of the full value of the shares. However, spreads can vary quite a lot and if you select an unusual or specialised investment trust you should ensure you are familiar with the spread because it can be as wide or wider than for a unit trust. However, you may have to contact a stockbroker for this information.

To calculate the value of a holding of investment trust shares multiply the price listed in the paper by the number of shares you own. To assess the performance of the investment compare this sum with the amount originally invested.

MASSAGED PERFORMANCE

One source of performance information is from investment fund operators. If you ask for information from one management company, perhaps having responded to an advertisement in a newspaper, you may be sent a graph showing that fund's performance. This can be useful. But statistics are easily manipulated and you need to be aware of the tricks used to make them seem better than they are.

Look to see what the parameters of the graph are and in particular watch the time-scale. The line graph representing the fund's performance may rise nicely, but if the time-scale is only a matter of months or a year or two you can rightly question the soundness of the performance record. More respect can be given to funds that can show sustained good performance over many years.

Individual fund performance is often compared with a benchmark, perhaps one of those discussed above. But assess the value of the comparison. For example, it is useful to compare an equity fund performance against inflation but it is hardly surprising that it beats inflation. Would not a comparison against the average performing investment fund be more telling?

Also look to see if an index measure has been calculated to include dividend income. Individual dividends from individual companies sound small but they mount up and compound growth rates impressively. The performance of a fund in capital terms is quite different from the performance in capital and income terms.

Yet because the income element is often forgotten about it is easy to make an individual fund's performance look much better than it is by comparing it with the capital element of an index measure. Newspapers and journals do not help battle against these kinds of misleading comparisons because they tend to print graphs showing the capital performance of indices, rather than the total return.

Special notice ought to be taken of dividend reinvestment by those people drawn to index-tracking funds and so-called guaranteed or protected funds. These funds have risen in popularity recently because they give a greater element of security to stock market investment but returns are often limited because the index measures used count only the capital element and ignore the effect of income via dividends.

Also watch for performance figures—particularly on the unit trusts side—presented on an 'offer to offer' basis, or a 'bid to bid' basis. The terms refer to the buying and selling prices of units, and a better indication of true performance is given if the spread between buying price and selling price is included. Therefore managers can make a fund's performance look better by comparing buying price at the start of the period with buying price at the end. A better measure would be to start with the buying price and end with the selling price. *Money Management* figures do this.

MINIMISE COSTS, MAXIMISE BENEFITS

Few things in life are free and nothing in finance comes gratis. There are always costs, some quite visible and some which are hard to quantify. Chapter 8 looks at charges on investment funds in some detail, but it is as well to mention them here as well because it is best to see costs in the context of performance. It is clearly best to pay as little in the way of charges as you can get away with. Charges are one of the most constant hindrances to investment growth, and can be seen as negative performance growth. However, good performance is worth paying for. If one manager can demonstrate the ability to produce better returns than rivals it may be justifiable for the manager to charge more than rivals.

By the same token it is good practice to make the most of any benefits that may be coming your way. Tax breaks are key and investment funds have them built in because there is no tax paid on investments made in the management of funds held in either a unit or an investment trust. Personal holding of investment funds can be sheltered from tax using PEPs, as described in Chapter 7. You ought also to be alive to any special bonuses or incentives—like cheap dealing fees—that may be offered to you.

Taxing Questions: Pepping up Your Prospects

Many collectives are sold in packages with personal equity plans (PEPs), the tax-friendly way to invest in collectives. This chapter describes what PEPs are and how they work. It looks at PEPs and collectives, which have grown in popularity side by side. It also assesses the dangers and attractions of PEPs and asks whether PEPs have real value or are merely a marketing ploy.

TAX FREE MEANS BIGGER PROFITS

Tax dodging is one of the best established and most keenly followed investor pursuits.

There is nothing illegal about most of the measures taken by individuals and institutions with the aim of avoiding the tax authorities. For most investors tax dodging is perfectly respectable. It is also attractive: because if you do not pay tax on profits, the profits are that much better.

Investors who use PEPs escape the obligation to pay income tax on any dividends received and capital gains tax on any rise in the value of an investment. However, unlike pension fund contributions which is the other significant and widely accessible tax break existing under the current system, all money saved in PEP investment comes out of taxed income.

Together with pensions, PEPs form today's two big personal investment tax breaks. PEPs were devised by Nigel Lawson during his time as Chancellor of the Exchequer and born in the Budget of 1986, introduced in 1987. PEPs quickly caught the public imagination. By April 1995, according to Inland Revenue statistics, £23.8 billion was invested in PEPs. Enthusiasm for PEPs has grown steadily since 1987 as Table 7.1 shows. Official numbers take a long time coming out but the indications are that the 1995–96 tax year saw the biggest ever movement into PEPs. New monies pledged between April 1995 and April 1996 were about £8 billion. Coupled with strong investment performance during that year the value of the total amount invested in PEPs has grown to about £40 billion.

The popularity of PEPs is well founded in common sense. The PEP tax breaks are valuable and can considerably advance the calibre of an investment. But it is vital not to get carried away by the tax-

Table 7.1   Growth of PEPs since 1987

Year	Number of subscribers	Amounts subscribed
1/1–31/12 1987	270 000	£480m
1/1–31/12 1988	120 000	£200m
1/1/1989–5/4/1990	580 000	£1.6bn
5/4/1990–5/4/1991	500 000	£1.6bn
5/4/1991–5/4/1992	750 000	£2.53bn
5/4/1992–5/4/1993	910 000	£3.49bn
5/4/1993–5/4/1994	1.59m	£6.32bn
5/4/1994–5/4/1995	1.62m	£5.9bn
5/4/1995–5/4/1996	2m (est)	£8bn (est)
Total	8.34m	£30.12bn*

Note * does not include investment growth

friendly aspect of any investment, and PEP investment funds are no exception. 'Do not invest for tax reasons' is an oft cited piece of investment wisdom, but one which is not always listened to. It is extremely important to keep the advantages presented by the tax authorities in perspective. After all, no tax dodge in the world will do any good if the underlying investment is a failure.

A PEP IS A TAX SHELTER—NOTHING MORE

Contrary to popular belief and contrary to the impression given by many investment fund advertisers and marketeers a PEP is not—strictly speaking—an investment. A PEP is nothing more than an official tax dodge. A PEP by itself has no intrinsic value, it is merely a framework which allows investors to earn investment profits free of tax.

A PEP is a tax shelter and is therefore only of use if the underlying investment makes money. The primary consideration must be to select a suitable and potentially profitable investment. If the underlying investment fails, the fact that profits are tax free is clearly of no use whatsoever. The decision whether or not to seek PEP status, a purely mechanical tax avoidance device, is secondary.

PEPS, A BRIEF HISTORY

Personal equity plans were dreamed up by Nigel Lawson for his Budget of March 1986 and were introduced at the beginning of the following year, just in time to catch the Black Monday crash of October 1987.

At first PEPs were designed to shelter from tax the profits derived from ownership of individual company shares. This, it was hoped, would promote direct investment in shares which in turn was seen as a roundabout way of supporting British firms, or at least those which were listed on the London Stock Exchange.

Between 1987 and the present the PEP allowance was gradually raised from £2400 to £9000. At the same time the rules were gradually relaxed so that the original idea of investment in individual company shares was changed to allow investment in pooled investment funds. You used to be allowed only to invest a small portion of the allowance in pooled investment vehicles but the proportion has grown. Now you can invest a maximum of £6000 a year—£500 a month—in PEP sheltered unit or investment trusts.

The nature of the PEP tax shelter has therefore changed. It was designed to encourage individual share ownership, and to make it more attractive for companies to raise capital from small investors. PEPs were designed as much to help companies as individuals but the emphasis has shifted: PEPs have now become a personal savings incentive. Government wants to reduce its obligations to provide welfare for people and it sees sense in giving tax breaks to those who are willing to save and protect themselves from future financial uncertainty.

PEPS, A BRIEF PROFILE

PEPs give protection from two taxes, income tax and capital gains tax. Income tax is collected before dividends are paid to investors so the PEP administrator has to reclaim the tax. Capital gains tax usually has to be paid when an asset is sold, and is calculated as a percentage of the growth in the capital value of the asset. PEP assets are simply taken out of the capital gains equation altogether.

You pay income tax at different rates on different bands of income. The income tax you normally have to pay on investment income is charged at your top rate. At current rates (December 1996) this could be either 40% for the well-off, 24% for middle-income earners, 20% or even 0% if you are in the lowest income bracket. The middle rate of 24% was reduced to 23%, for introduction in April 1997, by the Budget of November 1996. Capital gains tax is charged at an individual's top rate. It is these taxes you do not pay if you shelter assets in a PEP.

Each citizen over the age of 18 has a separate annual PEP allowance. Currently this is £9000 and is split into two parts. One portion of £6000 is called the general PEP allowance and a second of £3000 is called the single company PEP allowance. The underlying investment in a general PEP, as its name suggests, is broad. You can put it in a selection of individual company shares, corporate bonds and/or investment funds—either unit trusts or investment trusts. A general PEP is very flexible in terms of what assets are bought to slot into it. A single company PEP is less flexible. Again as the name implies, you are only allowed to put the shares of one company into a single company PEP. However, despite the fact that strictly speaking an investment trust is a single company, and for most purposes they are treated in the same way as normal companies, you cannot use a single company PEP allowance for investment in a single company PEP.

In each tax year every adult qualifies for a new PEP allowance. If you had subscribed the maximum amount in each tax year up to 1996–97 you would have put aside £64,200. A married couple could have squirrelled away twice that, and £128,400 is a small fortune in anybody's terms.

There is no time limit on PEPs. You do not have to hold a share or investment fund in a PEP for a certain time in order to qualify for the tax benefits. You can also trade the equity type assets held in a PEP, hold cash for a limited period of time, and transfer in shares received in rights and scrip issues.

PEPS AND INVESTMENT FUNDS

You can spend the entire £6000 annual general PEP allowance on investment funds. Individuals cannot administer a PEP themselves but have to employ an Inland Revenue authorised PEP manager, usually a stockbroking firm, a bank or investment fund administration company.

For investment fund investors there are two main approaches to PEPs. The simple way is to buy a packaged product where PEP status is automatically bolted on to the unit trust or investment trust you choose to buy. This ties you to one fund manager and may tie you to one fund, although some investment fund administrators will allow you to buy from a range of different funds they themselves have on offer. This kind of PEP arrangement is commonly called a managed PEP arrangement, and clearly limits your options.

Your choice is restricted to funds offered by the one fund manager/administrator. Also, if you do not want to invest up to the annual £6000 limit in the one place, but do have a total of £6000 to invest, you could waste part of the PEP allowance. This is because you can only own one PEP for every tax year and the allowance cannot be split between two separate PEPs. However, on the plus side the cost of managed PEPs tends to be low. Commonly the PEP edifice is added at marginal cost, and what charge there is is met from the annual fund management fees payable on the investment fund whether or not the PEP structure is erected.

The second approach is to use what are called self-select PEPs. As the name implies, these give consumers more flexibility and choice when using the PEP allowance. With a self-select PEP you can design a portfolio of different investment funds, from different fund managers. You could also slot in a couple of individual company shares and perhaps some corporate bonds as well.

You have to be careful that your investment qualifies under the rules, although the PEP administrator should be able to help and check out this sort of fine print. Qualifying investment funds have at least 50% of their assets in British or European Union companies—either shares or bonds. However, you can use one-quarter of your PEP allowance—£1500— for non-qualifying investments which have less than 50% of their assets in the shares or bonds of British or European Union companies.

If you wanted to you could self-select one investment fund for the PEP, although this would be a bit silly if the investment fund manager offered a managed PEP service, because it is likely that the packaged PEP would be cheaper.

PUTTING THE TAX BREAKS UNDER THE MICROSCOPE

It is a salacious prospect, earning investment profits and not even having to pay tax on the income and capital gains. But you ought not automatically assume that the benefits are as valuable as they seem. Under the current tax regime it is only those who are really quite wealthy, or who derive large amounts of income from stock market type investments, that actually need the tax protection provided by PEPs.

Each person has an annual capital gains tax allowance, currently set at £6300. That means— leaving PEPs aside—you have to secure capital growth of £6300 in a tax year before you pay capital gains tax anyway. That, for most ordinary wage earners, is far beyond what they might normally expect. Remember the £6300 allowance is also annual, so you are permitted that much tax-free capital gains in each and every tax year.

(Just to put it in perspective, a gain of £6300 would be achieved if an investment worth £31,500 rose in value by 20%. This is neither a small original investment sum nor a small rate of capital growth.)

For most people the tax exemption on dividend income has more relevance. It will kick in from the word go. However, the dividend income on many stock market investments is not generous so while you get income tax free, there is not a great deal of income to be had. Some kinds of investment—for example emerging markets and venture capital funds—are geared entirely to capital growth and there is no dividend income at all. Even where there is dividend income the administration charges on the PEP may be greater than the tax benefits.

A convincing argument can be constructed asserting that the PEP tax breaks cannot be as good as they sound because if they were the government could not afford to lose the tax income. So PEPs, it could be asserted, are nothing more than an elaborate confidence trick designed to get Britons to save more.

But then again saving is a thoroughly sensible thing to do, and if PEPs provide a marketing opportunity to get this message across to more people, why criticise them? Additionally, many investment fund managers build what is sometimes called the PEP wrapper around your investment for no visible extra charge. So unless you have better things to do with that PEP allowance you have nothing to lose by opting for the PEP option.

Furthermore the value of PEPs is increased the more income is earned. Therefore the relaxation in 1995 of the PEP legislation to allow corporate bonds to be eligible for inclusion in PEPs has made PEPs more useful. Corporate bonds are loans made by investors to companies and usually pay a better rate of interest than the equivalent yield from share dividends. In theory at least, the margin between the tax kicker and the PEP administration cost is that much wider. As the income from corporate bonds is that much better so is the value of getting that income tax free.

One other advantage of holding investments in a PEP is that it simplifies filling out tax returns. Investments held in a PEP, and the income deriving from them, do not need to be included on a tax return so there is an advantage in terms of end-of-tax-year paperwork.

THE GOVERNMENT AGENDA

In many cases central government positively encourages tax dodging by establishing and signposting loopholes with the aim of promoting a particular cause.

Recent British governments have given the owners of forests tax advantages because promoting the planting of trees was considered laudable. Investors in companies which run private nursing homes used to be able to tap into the favourable tax regime of Business Expansion Schemes because the government wanted to encourage private provision of this kind of health care. British film makers are constantly lobbying for tax breaks too, believing that their industry should get government support through the tax system.

In the recent history of personal investment in Britain government-sponsored tax dodging has targeted life insurance and home purchase. In fact, the current tax attractive PEP legislation promoting saving through shares and collective investment funds is only the latest in a line of comparable schemes. A future government may change the tax rules in accordance with a different political agenda. In the past Labour governments have taxed personal investment income more heavily and may

do so again. However, new governments rarely
withdraw tax breaks retrospectively so you can take
advantage of them where they exist with relative
equanimity.

Tax breaks for saving are likely to remain whatever kind of government there is. The logic of encouraging people to save more is compelling—both
from a government and personal point of view—so
it is highly likely that tax incentives will continue to
play a part in promoting saving. The way in which
the tax breaks are given may well change, however.
But the principal outline here in relation to PEPs can
be applied to tax breaks in whatever form they
should appear.

HANDLE TAX BREAKS WITH CARE

I couch some of my comments about PEPs in cau-
tionary language because many government-
sponsored tax dodges of the past have turned sour.
Two from the recent past, those on life insurance
policies and on home ownership, are worth detail-
ing because it is not beyond the realms of possibility
that PEPs will disappoint too.

Premiums on life insurance policies used to
escape tax. The government came to the view that it
was a good thing for individuals to have life insurance. If a wage earner dies it is sensible that some
financial provision is made to provide for surviving
dependants, perhaps a wife and children. Government could also justify the move because if private
provision is made for widows and orphans the Welfare State system—funded by taxes—would be
obliged to carry less of a burden. Similarly with
home ownership. The government subsidised home
purchase by making mortgage interest payments
tax deductible. Some of the logic was that if people
owned their own home the state, in this case local
councils, would have fewer people requiring rented

council accommodation. (There were other considerations too. Life insurance salesmen earned good commission from buyers which perpetuated their popularity. Margaret Thatcher as Prime Minister was politically motivated into using tax to encourage home ownership. She believed that home owners would naturally vote Conservative, and if there were more home owners there would be more chance of extending her term of rule.)

The logic which justifies the tax breaks in PEPs is that if ordinary people are encouraged to save they may have less reason to call on the state for financial support if they fall on hard times. It is also the case that by encouraging investment in shares in this way it means British companies are better supported financially. It is perfectly rational and sensible for governments to use the tax system in this way but my point is this. Both life insurance policies and home ownership became more popular than they should have done partly because investors concentrated on the tax breaks rather than intrinsic values. PEPs, too, may disappoint because too much emphasis is put on the tax angle, and not enough on choosing the underlying investment from where the value and growth come from.

As I have been at pains to make clear throughout this book, there are risks with stock market investment and the underlying investment assets in PEPs are stock market based. If you make a bad individual fund selection and it performs poorly the PEP structure will do nothing to help. If there is a more general, perhaps global, market crash the PEP regime will not offer any protection.

These are not reasons to avoid PEP investment because the framework has profit-enhancing merits. They are just warnings to make sure you invest for the right, sustainable, reasons. The popularity of life insurance linked endowment policies and residential housing was overcooked—partly by tax regime.

Expectations overtook reality and some disappointment ensued, but few patient and persistent investors were badly hurt. Similarly it is also hard to see
how PEPs would be undermined long term. A sud-
den fall in equity markets around the world would
give many less perceptive PEP investors a rude
awakening but history tells us that over time markets recover and progress forward. It is more important to choose a particular fund which promises
genuine growth. Do not expect a PEP to offer any
protection if you pick a poor performer.

In short, therefore, to invest for tax reasons
alone is dangerous. There is little harm, and some
good, done by accepting the benefits but there is a
bigger and more important picture to consider.

8 CHAPTER

Charged with Difficulties: Lies, Damned Lies, and Fee Structures

Fees and charges levied by investment managers can erode performance in startling fashion. But you cannot expect to be able to get involved in stock market investment unless you are prepared to pay some fees. This chapter explores the range of different types of fee—some obvious, others hidden. It also explains how managers justify the existence of fees, and how much investors should expect to pay.

Fees and charges are a pain in the neck. The structure on which management costs are built is invariably complex, and obtaining a full and clear picture is a difficult task.

Before I describe the intricate web of charges which apply—inconstantly—to all investment funds you should appreciate three basic points. The first is that the structure of charges incurred in the purchase of a unit trust is significantly different from an investment trust, although there are similarities too. The second is that charges inhibit performance. Unit trust companies, for example, often charge an initial fee of 5%. With a traditional unit trust, therefore, for every £100 you save only £95 is actually invested. This, quite clearly, is a serious restraint.

The third fundamental point to appreciate, however, is more positive. In paying fees to an investment fund manager you get access to the enhanced returns that often come with stock market type investment. You tap into professional fund management expertise and take advantage of the risk-spreading attractions of pooled investment.

Bear in mind that all types of investment carry charges. Just because a building society does not declare its costs in the same— usually visible—way of an investment fund, it does not mean charges are not levied. A building society, for example, merely pays less interest to savers and charges more to home buyers in order to earn its profit. This gap is a charge. If you invest directly into individual trading company shares there is the added cost of stockbrokers' dealing fees. You may also have to pay to get access to the information you need on which to base investment decisions. The time and effort expended by you making decisions are another cost.

Charges levied on an investment should be put in context of performance. It is better to pay 5% on an investment fund to achieve growth of 15%— giving a net positive growth of 10%—than it is to get a bargain deal of, say, 2% on a building society account which increases in value by 6%. In the latter case the net return is only 4%.

The collective investment fund method can be an economical and productive way to get more from your savings. But it is not sensible to abrogate all responsibility for investment. You should not simply hand over your money and forget about it. General investment policy decisions you should make yourself, even if you seek guidance from an adviser. You should also monitor performance and think about making changes if something happens in your life which makes change necessary or desirable. You should keep an eye on charges to make sure you get value for money.

Charges are an inevitable fact of investment life. There is no such thing as a free lunch, and if you expect to get something for nothing you will be disappointed. Bear in mind also that if you think you are getting something for nothing you are probably being deluded. The administration and fund management companies are not charities, they are commercial organisations with aims to make profits. Admittedly, the management companies' profit is your loss, but without enduring that loss you cannot partake in the potential handsome returns available from stock market type investments. Part of the skill of selecting an investment fund lies in choosing an investment fund manager where both he, and you, draw benefit.

CHARGING SCALES VARY

The scale of charges varies with the nature of the underlying investment. If a unit trust invests in bank deposits (money market funds do this) its charges should be low because the amount of work needed to find the best rates of interest are relatively modest. The same goes for the relatively new breed of funds known as **tracker funds.** These track a particular index measure—like the FTSE 100 or the FTSE All Share index. Operating a tracker is a largely mechanical process which can be carried out by computer. Once the program is set up trackers can almost run themselves with very little need of expensive, personal, human input. Money funds and tracker funds should be cheap to buy—with unit trusts of this type you should be able to get in with no initial charge and with an annual management fee of less than 1%.

More sophisticated funds, funds which require active management and the expense of time by

tracker fund: an investment fund which invests mechanically to mirror the composition of an index measure. The performance of a tracker fund will track the performance of the chosen index. Also called index funds.

highly paid professionals, cost more. However, the justification is that active management also means better management, and from that, in theory, comes better fund performance for you.

The debate between fans of trackers—where fund management techniques are said to be 'passive'—and more traditional 'active' fund management is hot. Tracker lovers say the added expense of active management invariably cancels out any additional performance benefits that may accrue. Active managers belittle trackers, because the traditional aim of investment has been to outdo the benchmark performance indices which trackers simply imitate.

The truth is that there is room to play it both ways. The more specialist the investment fund type, however, the greater the need for personal attention. At the other end of the spectrum from cash funds and trackers are venture capital trusts (VCTs). The underlying investments with VCTs are unquoted companies. Unquoteds are usually small, sometimes they are start-up situations, more often they are outfits which have been going a number of years but need investment in order to grow bigger. VCTs also commonly back management buy-outs, where the bosses of a subsidiary company in a larger concern break away. It takes a great deal of time and effort—and not a little skill—to identify companies in this bracket. It is even harder finding ones which represent a decent investment. Often VCT fund managers sit on the boards of the small companies in which investments are made. It is therefore not unreasonable that VCT administrators should be more generously rewarded for their input.

To an extent you get what you pay for. But it is a foolish investor who leaves the analysis at that. It is your money and you are the best person to ensure it is being looked after properly. If after a sustained period of underperformance with one manager you conclude another manager can do better for cheaper, it is your responsibility to swap. Where possible it is wise to go with a fund which offers performance-related incentives to managers in order to keep them on their toes. Performance-related fee structures are easier to set up with investment trust companies.

A final point to remember is that you are not always asked for a separate cheque for the fees. Quite often they are automatically deducted from the value of the fund. There is, therefore, a danger you may gloss over them, and forget the impact they have.

UNIT TRUSTS AND INVESTMENT TRUSTS: HOW CHARGES DIFFER

The most fundamental difference in the way charges are levied on a unit trust and on an investment trust is at the start and at the end of the time investors spend invested.

load: an investment or administration management fee.

If you select a unit trust you are hit with an initial charge which is quite usually at least 5%. This initial charge is sometimes called a 'front end **load**'. The charge—like many—is taken as a percentage of the amount you invest, so in pounds and pence terms the more you invest the greater the cost you incur. A large part of this 5% is marketing costs incurred by the unit trust company attracting you as an investor. It will pay a commission to a financial adviser of perhaps 3% out of this initial charge—if you were introduced to the group by an intermediary of this sort. If you go direct to the unit trust company it still imposes the full initial charge because, they say, they have paid to attract you in other ways. If you go direct the costs to the unit trust group are newspaper advertising and other forms of promotion.

While marketing costs are the biggest chunk of this initial fee other charges are included, perhaps most notably stamp duty. Stamp duty is a government tax levied on all purchases of equity investments at 0.5% of the purchase price.

The initial charge on a unit trust is not paid separately but mixed into the process of acquiring and disposing of units. There are two prices quoted for any unit trust at any one time. You can buy at a lower price and sell at a higher price with the gap between the two prices constituting the initial charge. The price at which an investor buys is called the 'offer' price. The redemption price is called the 'bid' price.

With an investment trust there is no such initial charge levied by the fund manager. For this reason investment trusts are often seen as being more attractive than unit trusts. The reasoning is simple: if you put £1000 into an investment trust you get £1000 worth of investment trust shares while if you put £1000 into a unit trust the value of your saving immediately drops to £950.

But the absence of an initial charge levied by the fund manager does not, unfortunately, mean there are no up-front costs associated with buying an investment trust. You have to pay a stockbroker to buy the investment trust company shares for you and the standard commission for this is 1.65%. Investment trust shares—like ordinary trading companies' shares, and unit trusts—are bought and sold at different prices. There is, to use the jargon, a 'bid-to-offer spread'. With an investment trust this is not usually as large as it is with a unit trust because it does not wind marketing expenses into it. It is more like the spread on bid and offer prices quoted for ordinary companies' shares, commonly between 0.5 and 1%. In addition you also have to pay the 0.5% stamp duty.

So if you add up all the expenses of buying an investment trust you get to 3%. So £1000 of investment will buy £1000 worth of investment trust shares, but you may have a separate bill for £30. The up-front cost is not an initial charge in the same way as with unit trusts and at 3% is still a smaller fee than is incurred with most front-end loading on unit trusts, However, the difference between the up-front cost of buying a unit trust and an investment trust is not as great as it at first seems.

UNIT TRUSTS AND INVESTMENT TRUSTS: HOW CHARGES ARE THE SAME

There are two big sets of charges paid on an investment fund. There are the fees incurred at the outset and there are those paid on an ongoing basis. The latter, commonly called annual management charges, are paid by both unit trust and investment trust investors. They vary from trust to trust and depend on how much work has to be done by managers, but are usually in the range of 0.5–2%.

Because annual fees are usually less than the initial charge on a unit trust, and less than the costs of buying investment trust shares, it is easy to think that the up-front costs are more important. This is not necessarily so. Compare two imaginary funds. Buying into the first incurs an up-front cost of 5% and it carries an annual management charge of 1%. Acquiring the second involves paying an up-front cost of only 2% but the annual fee is 2% as well. Which is better value?

It depends, of course, how long you invest for. If you invest for one year you pay 6% (5% plus 1%) on the first fund but 4% (2% plus 2%) on the second. If you invest for two years you pay another 1% on the first fund taking the total to 7% and another 2% on the second fund taking the cumulative figure to 6%. By year three the charges on the two funds are the same but by year four the charges on the second fund have overtaken the fees levied on the first and as time progresses further the gap widens quickly in favour of the first fund.

Investment in the stock market, as I have said before, needs time to show growth: five years is a benchmark minimum, and it often takes 10 years or more for equities to really prove outstanding value. It does not take a rocket scientist to work out that 10 lots of 2% are more significant than one lot of 5% plus 10 lots of 1%.

Furthermore, since the annual charge is levied as a percentage of the fund as it—hopefully—grows in value the 2% a year is not really comparable with the 5% initial fee. If the value of the fund does grow the amount of money you pay in annual management charges grows at the same time, even though the percentage levy stays the same. You have to have your wits about you in this game. A special offer waiving the initial charge may not be the bargain it looks if the annual fee is raised at the same time.

OTHER CHARGES TO BE AWARE OF

Exit charges are imposed if you decide to cash your investment chips in. They are only levied occasionally and are usually part of the same play-off between initial charges and annual management fees. They are sometimes called the 'back end load' and are often imposed in conjunction with the initial and annual management charges. Investment fund companies are at their most slippery when it comes to charges: one may promote itself with no front end load, only to slap a hefty back end load on. If this tactic is conjoined with a relatively high annual fee, you are stuck and stung for the displeasure.

Exit charges are by no means universal. In fact they are more the exception than the rule, and once again investment trusts have an edge here—back end loads are the preserve of unit trust companies.

The size of exit fee varies. It could be a fixed fee of around 3%. Alternatively, the scale could depend on how long you invest for. If you stick around for only one year you may get a 5% back end charge, stay two years and the exit fee is reduced to 4%, three years 3%, four years 2% and five years 1%.

Remember one other key point about exit charges. Percentage fees are calculated on the size of your fund at the time it is cashed in. So if you invest £1000 and it grows to be worth £1500 and you are paying a 3% exit fee, you will not pay 3% of £1000 (£30) but 3% of £1500—£45.

You may come across *switching fees* if you invest with a large fund manager who looks after several funds. As investors become more experienced they may like to switch between funds to change the direction or the emphasis of their investment exposure. If this is your intention you may be able to switch between the different funds under one manager's umbrella more cheaply than switching between two unconnected funds. However, some switching charge is usually levied.

Watch out for separate *personal equity plan* charges. Sometimes a tax-saving PEP structure will be added at no extra cost, but if there is extra to pay make sure that the cost of the PEP is less than the tax benefits you are likely to derive.

Check to see where the money comes from to pay annual management charges. Fees could be paid from capital invested in the fund or from the income earned by investments in dividends. Charges could be paid from both sources. It is particularly important to check this point when you invest in funds which provide regular income because you could get a false idea of how much income you receive, or how much capital you have left. As a rule it is better not to have fees taken from capital because the practice erodes the base from which future profits—both capital and income profits—are earned. If you are a capital growth seeking investor and you reinvest capital and income it does not make much odds whether the fees are taken from capital or from income. But if you take income out of the fund and fees are taken from capital your income is inflated at the expense of capital, which in turn has the effect of reducing the potential for earning income in the future.

You may have to pay an *income distribution charge* if you want to take income regularly.

DISCOUNT BROKERS

In the United States you can either be a 'load' or a 'no-load' investor. The load is levied as payment for advice and so it follows that no-load investors do not get advice, or pay for that advice separately.

In Britain the system has not developed that far. With the majority of funds you pay the loading whether or not you get any financial advice. The situation is changing, however, with the appearance of discount brokers who deal on what is commonly called an 'execution-only' basis. These are the equivalent of the American no-load funds. Unit trusts discount brokers simply rebate to customers some of the commission paid to them by the fund manager. The rebate is normally used to buy more units rather than be sent to you as a cash refund, however. For example, if you have £1000 to invest and the normal initial charge is 5% the discount broker might rebate 3%, so instead of investing £950 of the original sum you set out with £980 worth of investment.

If you are buying an investment trust and you are happy to make investment decisions yourself look for an execution-only share-dealing service rather than one of the traditional stockbrokers. Instead of the standard 1.65% dealing commission you may get away with half that. Also, if it is investment trusts you are after do not ignore dealing services run by the trust management company. It can gather together all buying requests from private investors and using the muscle that comes with having larger amounts of money, can negotiate reduced dealing rates with stockbrokers.

SHARE EXCHANGE SCHEMES

Many unit and investment trust companies will take individual companies' shares instead of cash by way of payment for a stake in the fund. Sometimes the fund manager takes the shares and adds them to the fund, other times the individual shares are sold and the cash used to buy either units in a unit trust or shares in an investment trust. The charge for share exchanges comes as a flat fee of maybe £15 or £20 or a percentage dealing commission. Occasionally fund managers run special offer periods where no charge is levied.

Share exchange schemes, particularly ones which carry no dealing charges, are good to take advantage of if you have just a couple of shares—perhaps inherited, or from buying into the privatisation issues. Using a share exchange scheme can be an economical way of broadening the base of your investment or changing its emphasis.

ACTUAL AND ALLOWABLE CHARGES

It is as well to be aware that a unit trust administrator may state that charges will be levied at a rate which is below the maximum allowed by the trust deeds. (The trust deed forms the legal framework document which ultimately controls what can and cannot be done by the administrators of the trust.) In theory, therefore, investors may be attracted in on one reasonable and attractive tariff of charges only to see those raised later on.

On investment trusts the annual management charges declared may not comprise the total charges levied on an ongoing basis. An investment trust company has other expenses such as paying its board of directors and organising annual meetings. These expenses are difficult to quantify without detailed reading of the report and accounts but in large trusts the sums involved are likely to be negligible compared to the amount of money being managed.

Regular Saving Schemes: Affordable, Flexible and Cheaper

Most investment houses run regular savings plans. How do these work? Also included is the theory behind pound cost averaging, and how it makes regular saving a cheaper way to invest. This chapter also emphasises and explains the wealth-building attributes of regular saving.

AFFORDABLE

Regular saving, as opposed to lump sum investment, has many advantages. But perhaps the greatest attraction is that regular saving makes stock market investment accessible to almost everybody. You do not have to be rich to invest in investment funds.

You do not need thousands of pounds but even low earners can make thousands of pounds. You can latch on to savings schemes where the minimum investment is as little as £20 a month. More commonly it is £50, and some houses have a minimum of £100 or more.

The mechanics of a saving scheme—and most investment fund management groups offer this

kind of small investor-friendly service these days—
are simple. You simply sign a standing order or
direct debit instructing your bank to send a set
amount each month off to the fund administrator.
The hard part is choosing which fund you want to
save with, but through reading this book you are
hopefully getting some idea of how to approach
fund selection.

FLEXIBLE

It is simple to set up a regular saving scheme and it
is also easy to stop contributions. Doing either is as
straightforward as writing to the bank and/or the
investment fund administrator and informing the
relevant people of your decision. Unlike less flexible
life assurance policies and some pension plans you
can start, stop, suspend or increase contributions to
an investment fund as you like. If you get made
redundant, become sick, lose income or need income for other purposes you can suspend contributions without penalty. If you get a pay rise or find
yourself with extra available cash you can increase
monthly subscriptions with as much hassle as it
takes to write a letter. You can also add larger lump
sums at irregular intervals.

Similarly, investment funds are flexible enough
to allow withdrawals. If you decide or are obliged
to dig into the fund at any stage you can do so
without cashing in the entire amount saved. This
flexibility compares very favourably with endowment policies—the life insurance/stock market
linked regular savings plans so often sold in conjunction with a home loan. With endowments you
are both heavily penalised for stopping contributions and obliged to sell out entirely if you want to
get anything at all back. Having said that it is not
wise to use an investment fund like a bank account
because undisturbed money grows at a better rate.

But the penalties should you decide on a reshuffle are much less onerous with investment funds, against comparable investment methods.

CHEAPER

Pound cost averaging works. The logical part of my mind says it should not, but it does work whether prices are rising, falling or meandering around a single point.

Pound cost averaging is an investment phenomenon which means it works out cheaper to invest at regular intervals than it does to invest lump sums. The mathematics are relatively straightforward but easiest explained in tabular form. A minute or two studying Tables 9.1–9.3 will tell the story better than words.

Table 9.1   Pound cost averaging—where cost price rises

Date	Price of unit/ share	No. units/ shares bought	Total cost
1 January	£0.50	200.00	£100.00
1 February	£0.51	196.08	£100.00
1 March	£0.53	190.11	£100.00
1 April	£0.54	185.19	£100.00
1 May	£0.55	181.82	£100.00
1 June	£0.56	179.53	£100.00
1 July	£0.57	176.21	£100.00
1 August	£0.58	172.41	£100.00
1 September	£0.59	169.49	£100.00
1 October	£0.60	166.67	£100.00
1 November	£0.61	163.93	£100.00
1 December	£0.62	161.29	£100.00
Average unit price	£0.56		
Total units bought		2142.74	
Cost at average price			£1205.38
Actual cost			£1200.00
Saving			£5.38

Table 9.2   Pound cost averaging—where price meanders

Date	Price of unit/ share	No. units/ shares bought	Total cost
1 January	£0.50	200.00	£100.00
1 February	£0.52	192.31	£100.00
1 March	£0.47	212.77	£100.00
1 April	£0.44	227.27	£100.00
1 May	£0.49	204.08	£100.00
1 June	£0.51	196.08	£100.00
1 July	£0.55	181.82	£100.00
1 August	£0.57	175.44	£100.00
1 September	£0.48	208.33	£100.00
1 October	£0.45	222.22	£100.00
1 November	£0.47	212.77	£100.00
1 December	£0.50	200.00	£100.00
Average unit price	£0.50		
Total units bought		2433.08	
Cost at average price			£1206.40
Actual cost			£1200.00
Saving			£6.40

However, what seems like mathematical magic is logically explained—like everything in finance, and all investments which work. It is simply that more unit trust units or investment trust shares are bought at the lower prices. And because the average price is higher than the lower prices, the average cost is inflated relative to the actual cost. But the fact that you can buy cheaply through regular savings schemes is more proof that numbers are easily manipulated than the basis of a sound investment strategy. It is a nice aspect, but in the final analysis the savings in pound cost averaging are small and theoretic. They are small in relation to the total amount invested, as the tables show. And they are theoretic because it is the closing value of the investment which really counts. It is that price, not the

Table 9.3   Pound cost averaging—where cost price falls

Date	Price of unit/ share	No. units/ shares bought	Total cost
1 January	£0.50	200.00	£100.00
1 February	£0.49	204.08	£100.00
1 March	£0.48	208.33	£100.00
1 April	£0.47	212.77	£100.00
1 May	£0.46	217.39	£100.00
1 June	£0.45	222.22	£100.00
1 July	£0.44	227.27	£100.00
1 August	£0.43	232.56	£100.00
1 September	£0.42	238.10	£100.00
1 October	£0.41	243.90	£100.00
1 November	£0.40	250.00	£100.00
1 December	£0.39	256.41	£100.00
Average unit price	£0.45		
Total units bought		2713.03	
Cost at average price			£1207.30
Actual cost			£1200.00
Saving			£7.30

theoretically improved acquisition cost, which determines whether an investment is good, bad or ugly. The savings are also theoretic because the actual cost is being compared to the average cost, and the latter number is by definition only a theoretic figure. Pound cost averaging may save pence, and if you look after the pennies the pounds take care of themselves. But you do need more.

TIMING

The more significant aspect of regular saving is that it smooths out the peaks and troughs of the investment roller coaster. Long-term returns are good but stock markets have an annoying habit of fluctuating in value over the short term. If you stage the purchase of an investment over time, however, you can reduce the impact of this volatility. Sometimes you will buy when prices are relatively high, other times prices will be relatively low, and most often prices will be somewhere in between. If you buy into an investment fund at a range of prices, therefore, you buy at an average and much fairer price.

Of course it is not all one-way traffic. If you compare the investment performance of £12,000 invested in a lump sum for 10 years against the end value of a 10-year £100 a month regular savings scheme the former will be better—assuming the performance of the investment fund chosen tracks an upward path. But this is because there is more money invested for more of the time.

But lump sum investment is not even an option for most people. One of the greatest attractions of regular savings schemes is that investors with little or no money saved up can build wealth. The great majority of people do not have inherited wealth, or are paid well enough to amass chunks of capital. But whoever you are it is a good idea to drip-feed money into stock markets.

THE MIRACLE OF COMPOUND GROWTH

Compound interest, or compounded growth rates, are sometimes called miraculous. They are not, of course, but the way in which **compounded growth** rates can work on the value of an investment fund can be astonishing. Compounded growth is so wonderful because it adds growth to growth. It therefore follows that the longer you save, the greater the overall compounded growth rate.

If you save £20 a month for a year—total sum invested £240—and the value of the investment grows at an annualised rate of 5% you will have a fund worth £246 at the end of the 12 months.

compound growth: growth in the value of an investment which benefits from growth in a previous period. Compound growth is, in effect, the calculated growth on growth together with growth on the original value of the asset.

(Annualised growth is growth over a full year. In this example most of the monthly contributions are invested for less than a year, so earn less than a year's worth of growth.) If you save £20 a month for five years (total sum invested £1200) and the growth rate is 5% a year the value of your investment will reach £1360. If you save on this regular basis for 10 years (total investment £2400) you will get £3105 and if you save over 25 years (total sum invested £6000) you will get back £11,910.

Over one year the element of profit as a proportion of the total amount invested is small. In this case it is £6 divided by £240 or 2.5%. But at the other end of the scale, the 25-year investment returns a profit of £5910 or 98.5% on the total amounts originally invested. It is this magnifying effect which gives compound growth rates the 'miraculous' label.

An average growth rate of 5% is not demanding. Most decent funds have in the past made this sort of return—averaged over five years or more—even after the negative effect of fees and charges has been taken into account. Good fund managers have turned in 7.5% annualised growth, and distinguished fund managers have achieved growth rates of 9% and more. However, it is as well to remember that investment growth rates bear more than a passing resemblance to rates of inflation. In the last 30 years or so investment growth rates have been high because inflation has been high. But if we enter a period of more controlled, lower rates of inflation it is likely that investment growth rates will adjust downwards too.

If in future inflation hovers at 2 or 3% managers who return more than 5% a year may be considered the top flight. But it is the growth achieved relative to inflation which is important, not the absolute growth rates. Table 9.4 plots the values of savings assuming various monthly contributions, saving periods and growth rates.

Table 9.4   Matrix of fund values with monthly contribution levels and annualised rates as variables

	5% AGR*	7.5% AGR	9% AGR	12%AGR
£50 per month for 1 year	£613.94	£621.06	£625.38	£634.13
£50 per month for 5 years	£3,400.30	£3,626.36	£3,771.21	£4,083.48
£50 per month for 10 years	£7,764.11	£8,896.52	£9,675.71	£11,501.93
£50 per month for 25 years	£29,775.49	£43,863.04	£56,056.10	£93,942.33
£100 per month for 1 year	£1,227.89	£1,242.12	£1,250.76	£1,268.25
£100 per month for 5 years	£6,800.61	£7,252.71	£7,542.41	£8,166.97
£100 per month for 10 years	£15,528.23	£17,793.03	£19,351.43	£23,003.87
£100 per month for 25 years	£59,550.97	£87,726.09	£112,112.19	£187,884.66
£250 per month for 1 year	£3,069.71	£3,105.30	£3,126.90	£3,170.63
£250 per month for 5 years	£17,001.52	£18,131.78	£18,856.03	£20,417.42
£250 per month for 10 years	£38,820.57	£44,482.59	£48,378.57	£57,509.67
£250 per month for 25 years	£148,877.43	£219,315.22	£280,280.48	£469,711.66

* AGR = annualised growth rate.

I also worked out that if you save £500 a month, for 35 years and achieve investment growth of 7.5% a year you will become a millionaire.

FROM LITTLE ACORNS

A glance at Table 9.4 shows how what seem like small changes can have a enormous effect. The difference between a growth rate of 7.5 and 9% may not seem significant but if you look at the sums you can see it makes a huge difference. Time is an even greater force. Save £100 for a year and you get a nice sum, save it for 25 years and you can pick up hundreds of thousands.

Doing these sums is complex because you are compounding growth of small chunks of money added at frequent intervals. Doing it by hand would be a thankless task involving hundreds of individual calculations. However, many home computer programs offer ready-made spreadsheet facilities that will compute compound interest for you. Then you can fiddle around with all sorts of monthly contribution levels, growth rates, terms and tax rates.

COLLECTION DATES

There are two points to bear in mind when getting involved with a regular savings plan. The first is to watch out for any exceptional charges levied by an administrator. The second is to be aware that managers usually aggregate all individual regular savings scheme contributions in a given month and make one block purchase of units or shares. There is a good reason for this which is that it would be expensive and time-consuming for the manager to make a succession of individual purchases for each different saver and in the long run all extra costs are picked up by the consumers.

But it is as well to check when a specific manager makes the block purchase. Then you can set up the standing order or direct debit instruction from your bank for a day or two beforehand. In this way you avoid a situation where your money might be hanging in limbo, and earning interest for the fund administrator rather than being invested and working for you.

THE NATIONAL LOTTERY—IT IS A LOTTERY

Perceptions about affordability are relative but £20 a month is within the reach of most earners. The average spend on National Lottery tickets is about £5—an outlay which is of course equivalent to more than £20 a month. Considering that upwards of 75% of the population regularly play this unsophisticated form of bingo it suggests that very many more people could use and benefit from investment funds than currently do.

Perception is a powerful force. But readers of this book should be in no doubt of my opinion which is that vast swathes of people have got their perceptions about investment seriously mixed up, especially when it comes to the National Lottery. Many believe you have to be well-off to invest in investment funds. As I hope I have demonstrated, this is not the case. Many are also scared by the risks involved with stock market investment. Yes, there are risks associated with buying investment funds but these pale into insignificance beside the risks associated with investing in National Lottery tickets.

A worryingly large number of people, I believe, think of the National Lottery as investment. They may not admit it, but observation and anecdotal evidence strongly suggest they do. I regularly come across people who spend significant amounts of money on the Lottery in the hope and expectation of winning unfeasibly large amounts of money.

And they must *expect* to win. If you are in it for the cheap thrill—and there is nothing wrong with having a bit of fun—you need buy no more than one ticket, and spend no more than £1. But there are people around who lay out tens of pounds a week. If the jackpot is unwon one week, and rolls over to the following draw, people start 'investing' many tens of pounds, buying 50 or more tickets.

The investment concept, of pledging money in order to get more money back, is one shared by stock market investors and National Lottery players. But perceptions are skewed. National Lottery players run the acute risk of losing all their money. Investment fund investors, however, have only a small chance of losing their stake and a very good chance of making profits.

Remember the odds on Lottery tickets. It is about 14 million to 1 that you hit the jackpot, and about 50 to 1 that you win the minimum £10 prize.

Looked at another way, that means 49 times out of 50 you will lose everything, and there are 13,999,999 chances out of 14 million that you will *not* win the big prize. The odds against you are just unfeasibly large. There is a 2500 times greater statistical chance you will die in a week before a Lottery draw than you will win the jackpot.

The odds on investment fund prospects cannot be calculated so simply. But if you invest in the average performer for a period of five years or more, and assume that the future will mirror the past, you can be almost sure you will get your money back. Figures 6.1 and 6.2 show what the odds of winning are if you invest in an investment fund whose performance mirrors the FTSE All Share index. They are extremely good.

IT IS NO JOKE

An element of fun should be enjoyed by both investment fund investors and National Lottery players, but the proportionate importance of serious money making and entertainment must be got right. The economics of the Welfare State are slowly but surely becoming unravelled, making it increasingly important for more people to make private provision for their futures. Unemployment, sickness, maternity, disability, pensions, geriatric nursing home care are all expensive and the politicians—of all hues—will not be able to sanction financial support from the state which will provide anything more than a subsistence level standard of living.

Principles of Good Fund Management: How and What to Learn from the Professionals

This chapter outlines the principles of investment management to help investors understand what the managers do. At the same time it equips them with tools to be able to make necessary investment decisions themselves.

If you are to make money successfully you have to learn the secrets of the investment management trade. One of the advantages of investing in collectives is that you pay someone else—a professional—to do the day-to-day money management. However, it is best to have a grasp of those basic principles in order to make informed choices about whom to select as your investment manager, and in order to monitor your investments sensibly.

You need to grasp the essential principles to make the most elementary choices between funds. As you gain experience you may be inclined to accept more responsibility for investment management decisions. This is possible with investment funds. It can also add excitement and enjoyment to the investment process. In addition, the criteria for selecting funds are not that different from selecting between individual shares. With experience you can use the following set of principles to broaden your portfolio. It will be useful to acquire investment management expertise because as you become more advanced, you may want to spread your wings and buy some shares in individual companies.

It may be relevant to remember that investment funds are used heavily by full-time professional fund managers. Collective investment vehicles like unit or investment trusts make up one part—an important part—of many sophisticated and well-rounded portfolios.

BUY LOW, SELL HIGH

The secret of every investment manager's success is to buy cheap and sell dear. It is the basis of every successful business too, for that matter. The formula is simple, and it is even tempting to ignore it as a fatuous truism. Yet month after month, year after year, private investors choose to fall foul of this simple maxim. Figure 10.1 plots UK unit trust purchasing activity against the performance of the FTSE All Share index. It is uncanny how peaks of buying coincide with times when the index is rising strongly and nearing the almost inevitable correction. It is similarly unnerving how the troughs of purchasing activity match periods when stock prices are meandering. At times when prices are high investors should not be buying: but they do. When prices are low investors keep away, but history suggests that is exactly when they should be piling in.

To be a 'contra-cyclical' investor, that is to invest against the general economic and stock market trends, is sound investment strategy. It also applies to individual funds and groups of funds which fall

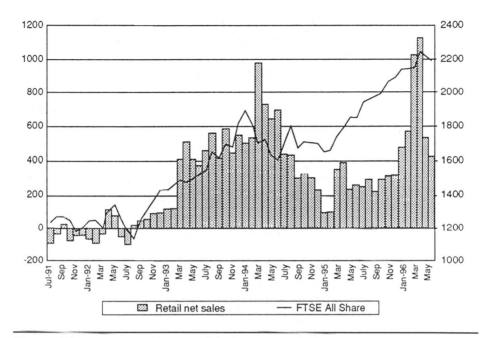

Figure 10.1   Unit trust sales figures compared to FTSE All Share Index. Source: AUTIF

in and out of favour. But you should also look for value too. Just because an investment is cheap does not necessarily make it a bargain. Other investors may have passed over the opportunity to invest for very good reasons. A little contra-cyclicality, therefore, is a good thing but you should be careful not to be too obtuse. If you ignore altogether what other investors are doing you can miss out. If lots of money chases stock, the price of the stock rises. It does not matter—at least not in the short term—whether the rise is justifiable. All that matters at the end of the day is that an investment is appreciating in value and if you are in it you are getting richer and if you are out of it you are not. These demand-led increases are sometimes said to be caused by 'weight of money'.

   Japanese private investors—in their millions— spent the 1980s saving relatively small amounts of money into stock market investments by automatic debit on a monthly basis. Individual amounts may have been quite small, but the collective amount of money flowing into the Japanese market became enormous. Month after month, hordes of small investors bought small numbers of shares, with the result that constant upward pressure was put on share prices. This was an inevitable consequence as the first law of economics, that of supply and demand, worked itself through. Demand for shares was constantly strong but supply of shares was limited, therefore the price of shares moved up regardless of what was happening in the real world.

Share prices moved to stratospheric levels until the collywobbles struck, as they often do. The higher share prices rise, the further they fall. In Japan private investors withdrew, taking their small monthly savings elsewhere, and suddenly the law of supply and demand worked in reverse. There was loads of supply, and little demand, forcing share prices to sink.

Weight of money also goes some way to explaining why markets are volatile and why people invest when markets are rising to near peaks but do not invest at the better times, when markets are in the doldrums. In prosperous times people have money to spend and save and part of it is directed into stock market investments. In leaner times, however, the money is not in people's pockets, available for investment.

Investment trust investors have an opportunity to look for value not afforded by unit trust investors. As explained in Chapter 3, the price of an investment trust's shares rarely reflects exactly the value of the underlying assets held in the investment fund. Occasionally the shares trade at a premium to net asset value (NAV) per share, that is the shares are priced higher than the NAV. Mostly, however, investment trust shares are said to trade at a discount to NAV.

If the shares trade at a discount to NAV and you buy the shares you are, in effect, buying assets cheaply. The trouble is that NAV discounts widen and narrow according to barely comprehensible laws, so while you may buy assets cheaply you may find them on offer even more cheaply later on. If you have the skill and the luck, however, you may be able to find investment trusts where discounts may narrow. In other words, you may find value.

In the *FT* the list of prices of investment trusts is accompanied by a figure which shows the size of the NAV discount, or premium. A number is printed in the final column which represents the percentage discount or premium but confusingly it is premium percentages which are prefixed by a minus sign. If the figure does not have a minus sign it represents a discount.

SET CLEAR BUT FLEXIBLE GOALS

All investors should have goals. Before taking the plunge ask yourself what is the aim of the investment you are about to make. Having a clear aim will make it easier to select a fund but it will also serve a useful purpose when it comes to reviewing a particular investment. If, for example, your aim is to invest in order to have enough money to pay for a daughter's wedding you will want a fund that delivers capital growth because to pay for the wedding you need a lump sum of cash. Keep that aim in mind during the period of an investment because it becomes a touchstone.

An investment ought to be reviewed at least quarterly, preferably monthly. If at any stage you find that you have invested enough and won sufficient investment returns to pay for the wedding, you can pull out and pop the accumulated sum in a building society ready for the nuptial bills. It depends on how much time you have, but if you leave an investment untouched in the hope of greater returns, you may be disappointed by a stock market slump.

An investment aim does not need to be as specific as the desire to pay for a wedding. It can be as vague as just wanting a bit more money. But it is important to set down an objective so that when it comes to making your regular investment review you can ask yourself: Have I achieved what I set out to do? If the answer is yes, that is an excellent reason to finish or change an investment programme. There is one age-old share-dealers' maxim which will never sound old-fashioned. It says 'always leave something for the market' and it means, get out while the going's good.

It is advisable to have clear objectives about the downside too. You have to be prepared to stomach losses from time to time, but it is sensible to predetermine how much loss you are prepared to handle. Once you meet or exceed that loss, get out. The objectives you set in regard of the profits and losses must be related to the kind of fund you invest in. If you chose a high-risk, high-reward fund you can allow yourself to be more ambitious on the upside but at the same time you must be prepared to see the value of your investment fall more than you would ordinarily like. If a low-risk, low-return fund starts falling in value alarm bells should start ringing quickly.

It is extremely important to be realistic about stock market investment. No one, not even the best respected and highest paid professional investment managers, can spot the bottom of the market and buy, while being able to pinpoint the very top of the market and sell. The most anyone can do is to buy when prices are relatively cheap and sell when things are, by and large, pretty good.

BOTTOM UP OR TOP DOWN

This is jargon for the two different ways you can approach investment in company shares. It is useful to know what the jargon means because it is often used to explain a particular fund manager's investment strategy. You can also apply it to the process which you might go through during the selection of a fund or a range of funds.

A 'bottom-up' approach is where an investment manager will pick a particular company's shares because he or she has researched the prospects of the company and thinks that it and its shares will do well. Investment decisions are made on what is sometimes called a 'stock-specific' basis. A 'top-down' approach to investment is quite different. A devotee of the top-down approach will look at nations or geographic regions, and make investment decisions on how well or badly he or she thinks the whole economy will fare. Individual stock selection is a secondary matter because, according to top-down logic, if the economy which forms a particular company's market is not healthy it is very much more difficult for an individual company to succeed. The shares bought by the top-down investor are usually the largest companies or a selection which should broadly reflect the performance of the stock market in question.

Of course, the best fund manager will be the one who buys the most promising stocks in the most promising geographical areas and most fund managers do synthesise elements of both approaches in the execution of investment practice. But one or other approach may be favoured.

If you are investing in funds you could ask yourself similar questions. If you are by inclination a top-down sort of investor you may like to invest in stock markets serving geographical regions which you believe hold promise of economic prosperity. If you are more taken by the bottom-up approach you may prefer funds which specialise in investing in particular industrial sectors or types of company. You may want both.

THE IMPORTANCE OF MANAGEMENT

Management skills, or lack of them, are one of the leading influences on a professional investor's mind when he or she is making an investment decision. The fortunes of a company, and a company's share price, are closely linked to the talent of senior executives. The quality of an investment, therefore, is to an extent dependent on the quality of management. If senior executives can display good judgement, innovate where appropriate, motivate staff, see opportunities for gain and spot trouble before becoming too embroiled, the chances are that the company they are charged with running will be a good one.

For the private investor using investment funds some attention, therefore, should be paid to a particular fund manager's ability to spot well-run companies. This is not easy: an investor will have to be a dedicated reader of the financial press to be able to judge management ability and be able to cross-refer to the individual companies bought and sold by a fund manager. In the investment fund arena management skill is particularly important when a choice is being made between the shares of companies. Fund managers who invest on a bottom-up or stock-specific basis will be particularly keen to identify top-notch management. The talents of particular company executives are less important to those investing in bonds or bank deposits, for example.

Perhaps more important to the private investor, however, is the broader principle that managers have a large influence on investment performance. Investment fund managers have every bit as much influence over the fortunes of a fund as the senior executives have over the prosperity of a company.

Picking quality management is vital but as with many of the most critical influences in this sphere it is also one of the hardest to tie down and quantify. You should, however, look out for changes of fund manager as reported in the press and in the half-yearly reports sent to you. You should also bear in mind that while a fund management company may not change, individuals at the fund management company may. Considering that individual fund managers as much as fund management companies actually handle money in a fund, changes in personnel can be as important as changes in fund management company.

RESEARCH COUNTS

Good fund managers also research hard. In all investment there is an element of guesswork, but if proper and thorough research is undertaken the element of guesswork can be limited. Where guesses have to be made they can be informed guesses or estimates rather than wild stabs in the dark. You should keep abreast of news events, study economic and stock market statistics, and performance indicators. And good research is not confined to poring over numbers all the time. It can be just as important to be aware of political changes and of social trends and to be able to relate real world activity to investment. Investment does rely to a certain extent, after all, on what real world consumers do with their time and money.

SEE BOTH SIDES

It is easy to get carried away with an argument in favour of making a particular investment, or indeed be too comprehensively negative about a situation. You may develop a line of argument which makes a particular investment seem impossible to turn away from. But it is also easy to be deluded by slickly presented investment arguments—either those generated yourself or by those pushed at you by advisers and investment marketeers. Indicators very rarely point one way and one way only and if they seem thus, you are probably missing something. There will be plus points and minus points in any piece of investment logic.

MOTORS FOR GROWTH

Many factors act upon an investment to determine whether it turns out well, badly or indifferently. Two factors, however, drive the fortunes of economies and companies more than most: technological advances and population growth.

Companies need markets in order to sell the goods and services they make and provide. New markets are created and expanded largely because of new technology or through population growth. For instance, the invention of computers created an enormous market for people who designed, manufactured and sold computers. Similarly one of the most exciting economic areas in the world at the moment is South East Asia, and part of the reason for that is that the number of people living in the region is expanding. More people means more consumers and that means a new or bigger marketplace. The opening up of previously closed populations—like China and Eastern Europe—has a similar effect in economic terms as an actual increase in the birth rate.

THE BALANCE OF PROBABILITIES

The last point to appreciate about fund management is that things rarely make absolute sense. If you have been confused reading this chapter, and thought that several points directly contradicted others, it is not surprising. Several points do contradict others. But investment is like this. It is chaotic. The good investor will be able to handle contradiction and chaos, distil what are the most important factors to consider and make a judgement dependent on the balance of probabilities.

Weight Patiently: Asset Allocation and Time Horizons

This chapter outlines the principle of building a portfolio of collective investments. It stresses the importance of knowing what risk is and knowing what kind of appetite you have for it. It also examines the realistic time horizons needed to achieve returns and how an individual's time constraints—that is, is the investor a pensioner, a saver for school fees, a young speculator—should affect investment decisions. The healing effect of time on successive stock market crashes will also be discussed.

RISK/REWARD: THE FIRST LAW OF INVESTMENT

In the campaign to invest successfully it is vital to understand the relationship between risk and reward. Until you have an idea of what risk means, and can grasp the real value of rewards, you cannot hope to make sensible investment choices.

Think of the risk/reward principle like a law of physics. Where a student of gravity will happily observe: 'What goes up must come down,' a good investor should notice: 'The greater the risk of loss the greater the reward in profit. The less the risk of loss, the less reward in profit.'

Risk and reward perform as a double act. They move, generally speaking, in tandem. To establish an understanding of risk and reward look at the simple line graph in Figure 11.1. Where the axis lines cross is ground zero, the neutral point where there is no risk, and no reward. As you track up the vertical, risk of loss increases. As you move out to the right on the horizontal, the likelihood of reward increases. You could, if you had suitable measures of risk and reward, plot all different kinds of investment on this chart. If you did, sensible and realistic ones would sit on, or near, the dotted diagonal line because it is the dotted diagonal that represents the point of balance between risk and reward. This is the line of investment equilibrium. Positions high and to the left are no good because no one wants lots of risk of loss and little potential for profit. Positions low and to the right—where low risk meets high reward—are the stuff of dreams.

Investments such as would occupy a low-risk/high-reward position are not commonly available to inhabitants of the real world. Incidentally, however, because the proposition is so attractive it is also the kind of invitation commonly used to lure unwary investors into unsustainable or fraudulent investment schemes.

THE RISK/REWARD SPECTRUM

Unlike many laws of physics, however, the first law of investment is not rigid. Investment is not an exact science. The relationship between risk and reward is a dynamic one, it is flexible and elastic. You can also liken the risk/reward relationship to a spectrum. In different investments the amount of risk,

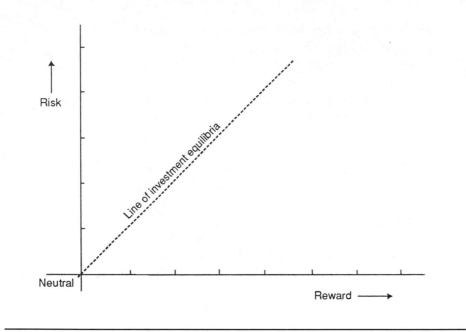

Figure 11.1   Risk/reward line graph

and the amount of reward, change gradually. Emphasis shifts and boundaries are blurred.

Investment fund investment only occupies a segment of the spectrum. There are savings vehicles that exist beyond the range of investment funds and within their range. To illustrate the spectrum analogy look at Table 11.1 on pages 172–173. It was drawn up by Premier Investment Management, a firm of independent financial advisers. At the top are safe investments, ones which are low risk, low reward. At the foot of the chart are high-risk, high-reward investments.

RISK AND VOLATILITY

Premier defines risk as volatility in construction of its risk rankings. Riskier investments tend to move more sharply in price and if a price moves up and down wildly the risk of selling at a bad time is increased. Volatility is relatively simple to measure as well, so it is easy to define risk as volatility. However, the relationship between risk and reward does not stop at volatility.

Risk means more than the likelihood that the value of an investment will fall in price. The effect of inflation on the value of an investment must also be taken into account. As Figure 6.4 shows, the value of money falls—in inflation adjusted 'real' terms—if you take a very cautious stance—that is you invest only in, say, building society deposits. The relationship between risk and reward shifts so that the risk assessment becomes not what the actual value of a pot of money is but how effectively that money retains its buying power. Time and inflation change the way risk should be assessed: over long periods there is a very real risk that the buying power of money saved in a building society deposit will erode. Yet the risk that an equity based investment will lose real value is much smaller.

Investors who ignore the erosive effects of inflation and do not appreciate the potentially damaging impact of adopting an ultra-cautious approach to investment have a name. They are called 'reckless conservatives'.

KNOW YOUR OWN APPETITE

You have to assess your own attitude to risk and reward before you can make any decent investment decisions or be able to build a portfolio of investments. You have to decide how you, personally, fit into the equation. If you hate the idea of losing money but can live with the thought that you may not make much, you are a very different kind of investor from the person who is willing to take a chance and hope to see the value of their savings increase nicely.

It is vital not to underestimate the importance of time, too. Some investments need more time to

Table 11.1   Risk–reward table. Source: Premier Investments

Group 1	1 National Savings
	2 Bank/building society deposits
	3 Short-dated British government gilts
	4 Cash unit trusts
	5 Gilt and fixed interest unit trusts
	6 Offshore managed currency funds
	7 Diversified gilt portfolios
Group 2	8 International fixed interest unit trusts
	9 Offshore global fixed interest funds
	10 Medium-dated British government gilts
	11 Diversified offshore fund portfolios
	12 Insurance company mixed funds
	13 Offshore managed funds
Group 3	14 Long-dated British government gilts
	15 Insurance company mixed pension funds
	16 International equity and bond unit trusts
	17 International equity income unit trusts
	18 Insurance company international funds
	19 Fund of funds unit trusts
Group 4	20 Diversified unit trust portfolios
	21 Insurance company equity funds
	22 Insurance company international pension funds
	23 UK equity and bond unit trusts
	24 Offshore global equity funds
	25 UK capital growth investment trusts
Group 5	26 Venture and development capital investment trusts
	27 European unit trusts
	28 UK equity and bond unit trusts
	29 International equity growth unit trusts
	30 Offshore UK equity funds
	31 Insurance company UK equity pension funds
Group 6	32 UK general investment trusts
	33 UK equity income unit trusts

34 FTSE 100 total return (index)
35 Investment trust unit trusts
36 UK growth and income unit trusts
37 Financial and property unit trusts

Group 7   38 FTSE smaller companies (index)
39 UK equity growth unit trusts
40 UK smaller company unit trusts
41 High income investment trusts
42 Smaller companies investment trusts
43 European investment trusts

Group 8   44 UK income growth investment trusts
45 FTA All Share total return (index)
46 Diversified investment trust portfolios
47 International general investment trusts
48 Far East (incl. Japan) unit trusts
49 North American unit trusts

Group 9   50 FTSE Mid 250 (index)
51 Japanese unit trusts
52 Property unit trusts
53 North American investment trusts
54 Commodity and energy unit trusts
55 Far East (excl. Japan) investment trusts

Group 10   56 Far East (incl. Japan) investment trusts
57 Japanese investment trusts
58 Far East (excl. Japan) investment trusts
59 Emerging markets investment trusts
60 Commodity and energy investment trusts
61 Investment trust warrants

mature than others. An investor's time requirements exert great influence over where he or she should be positioned in the risk/reward spectrum. If you need a place to put money for just a few months it is probably not sensible to save in stock market type funds because up-front costs can erode value and short-term price movements can be downwards. If the time horizon is months it is better to stick with a deposit account where you will retain the value of money and should earn a bit on it too. If you are prepared to wait years, on the other hand, the costs of investment should be outweighed by the returns. The very strong message from history is that if you have time you should invest in stock market type investments because average long-term returns are much better than from deposits. It is a message covered in detail in Chapter 6, and illustrated in Figures 6.3 and 6.4.

Younger people are usually better placed to take on more risk because they have the time to allow investments to mature. Older people, on the other hand, may need to live off money already saved so may want to adopt a more cautious approach. If you are saving spare cash in the hope of buying yourself a flash sports car you may be prepared to invest in a fund with a high risk/reward profile because the need you are trying to satisfy is not essential. If you are saving to pay for a child's education, however, a steadier investment selection may be wiser.

SPREADING RISK AND REWARD

It is not an accident that the saying 'don't keep all your eggs in one basket' is as old as the hills. It is eminently sensible, timeless advice which is applicable to many situations in life. It is an adage that takes an honoured seat at the dining table of investment wisdom.

Any investor buying a collective investment automatically adheres to the maxim. Indeed it is their in-built compliance with the eggs-in-one-basket advice that is one of the main reasons why unit and investment trusts are so popular. In selecting one fund, participants actually choose a spread of investments. In the quaint language of the age-old adage, saving with investment funds means that precious nest eggs are placed in a series of different hidey-holes as a matter of course. Some of the eggs may go rotten, others will survive and flourish. But overall, and given enough time, this protective strategy should prove itself to be a productive one. It is not enough to stop there, however. Some funds are more protective than others. Managed funds, funds of funds and broadly based international funds divide the eggs between as wide a range of locations as any. No investment fund is entirely immune from violation, and many are a good deal more susceptible to unpleasantness than the promoters would have you believe. Country- or region-specific funds are vulnerable and funds invested in one particular industry are in a similar position. Risk is spread with these higher-risk funds but the effectiveness of the protection mechanism is relative to the greater level of risk that is shared by the range of investments included in the fund.

There is nothing inherently wrong with high-risk funds. Indeed the attractive profit prospects means there is a lot right with them. They must simply be used by the right people. An adventurous but sensible investor will buy several different high-risk funds as insurance against the possibility of failure in one or two. It is also wise to balance high-risk investment with exposure to funds in the lower-risk bracket. The loading of high-risk and low-risk funds depends on how adventurous or cautious you are.

In short, investment funds are ready-made diversified portfolios. But some are more diversified than others. The Premier table includes all sorts of investment types so allows you to get a feel for the broader picture.

BUILDING A PORTFOLIO

You can build a sound, well-balanced portfolio of collective investments by buying a fund of funds (FoF), a managed fund or a broadly based international fund. The benefit of an international fund over an FoF is that you only pay one set of management charges. Either option, however, can be used by first-time investors who are unsure of what they are getting into, and want to start with the most general sort of investment possible. More experienced investors, however, and those who have built up some capital with a broad fund, might want to design and build their own portfolios. This is done by investing in several unit or investment trusts, with the idea that each investment plays a different role in the campaign to meet an overall objective.

The great advantage of designing your own portfolio is that you can assess your needs much more accurately than an outsider, and you can establish a portfolio to meet those needs much more closely. It is also more fun, and more rewarding than letting someone else do it. It is also largely a myth that you need the specialist knowledge of a highly paid City financier to produce results. Respectable studies have been undertaken which demonstrate that a baby with a crayon and a copy of the prices page of the *FT* can pick as good a selection of shares as many professionals. Of course, and like many things in this field, the opposite is equally true. Professionals can produce results which are every bit as good as a blind monkey.

The exact make-up of a portfolio depends on personal circumstances and personal preference but many people may elect to keep a core of investment in a broadly based fund, say 50%. If you are a pensioner and want income you may decide to invest that core in an income-biased general fund or one where you can receive regular payments. The other 50% could be divided between three, four or five more specialist funds. One or two may be more cautious bond funds. Others may give you an exposure to Far East growth markets, or smaller companies, or a particularly exciting industrial sector: technology companies for example.

Younger people may view the money they have to invest in investment funds as the higher-risk element of an overall saving strategy. Pension savings, invested in a managed fund, may take care of the core element and suitable investment funds to be bought may be all in the higher-risk categories. If you do not have a lump sum to carve up and invest, but instead want to build capital using regular savings schemes, you may select one steady fund at first then start other saving schemes with different investment aims, perhaps managed by different companies. Some fund management groups will allow you to set up one direct debit but give you the choice of how to split that money between a range of the funds it manages. You may want to change the split over time and you can do that too.

It is difficult and could be misleading to make too many generalisations about how a portfolio should be built. Every individual's portfolio will differ because every individual is different. Below, however, are some example portfolios for some typical—but imaginary—people drawn up by Jonathan Fry of Premier Investment Group.

Case 1

Man or woman, age 28, single with £100 a month to save. Is prepared to invest for five years or more and is willing to accept medium to high risk. Has no particular plans for money.

May consider establishing two separate investment fund savings plans. One, for £50 a month, could be a generalist fund which qualifies for PEP tax sheltering. The other £50 a month could go into a higher-risk special situation investment fund like emerging markets. Would want a non-contractual arrangement where it is easy to halt payments if required.

Case 2

Man or woman, age 28, single with £15,000 legacy. Wants to invest for three to five years and is willing to accept medium to high risk. Has no particular plans for money.

He or she may think about investing £5000 into a diversified, that is broadly spread, generalist investment fund and once again target one based in the UK or Europe in order to qualify for PEP status. The remaining £10,000 could be split between two or three more specialist investment trusts or unit trusts, for example in the Far East, Japan or America, or in a technology fund. May try to spread investment across two tax years so that more of the investment is sheltered from tax by using two successive PEP allowances.

Case 3

Married couple age 35, with a £5000 bonus payment from husband's job, and £100 a month to invest. Looking to save for 5–10 years with a wedding, school fees or a change of house in mind. Medium risk.

A diversified, broad-based investment fund again provides the core holding. It could be a FoF unit trust or investment trust perhaps allied to a PEP. Half the £100 monthly also invested cautiously in a generalist investment fund savings scheme with a UK bias, where volatility is less of a problem. The other £50 to be more aggressively invested in a Far East fund, including Japanese exposure. The couple should review the arrangement every tax year to take advantage of new PEP allowances and to spread investment across different sorts of specialist funds and between different fund management houses.

Case 4

Divorced woman age 40, with a £25,000 divorce settlement. Sees money as a substitute pension so is willing to invest for 20 years or so. Wants a medium risk.

She might like to split money in six parts. The overriding concern is to create a sufficiently diversified portfolio in order to spread the risk and gain exposure to a variety of different investment mediums as the client needs to have maximum capital growth and take advantage of a range of investment opportunities. So four tranches of £5000 would be directed towards (A) international equity unit trust, (B) UK capital growth investment trust, (C) a venture capital investment trust and (D) a Far East including Japan unit trust. Two lots of £2500 may be risked in (E) an emerging markets investment trust and (F) a fund of investment trust warrants.

She might like to spread her investment across several tax years in order to run less risk that she pledges all at a time when world stock markets are expensive and perhaps due for a correction. This would allow her to shelter more of her investments from tax using PEP and venture capital trust tax breaks. If she wants to keep money on deposit awaiting investment she might use a cash unit trust.

Case 5

Retired couple in early sixties who have £40,000 to invest. They want capital growth and are looking to stay invested for most of the rest of their lives which they hope will be 20–25 years. They only want medium to low risk and the ability to turn capital into income if required.

To secure capital growth with low risk consider putting £15,000 in an FoF unit trust or an investment trust of investment trusts. The other £25,000 might be invested in £5000 tranches into five different funds with varying low- to medium-risk profiles starting with a fixed interest fund (perhaps a corporate bond PEP) and moving up in risk to an income fund where dividends are reinvested, a balanced UK equity fund, and a balanced international fund. Husband and wife have separate PEP allowances and investment could be phased to take full advantage of their £12,000 joint quota.

Case 6

Retired couple aged 65 with £25,000 to invest and need maximum income. Medium to low risk again and are looking at 15–20 years.

Would consider a portfolio of zero dividend preference shares and split capital investment trusts to give above average income. May also consider a portfolio of income-generating investment funds which also have capacity for capital growth.

Case 7

Widow, age 75, with £20,000 to invest to cover or at least help towards the cost of nursing home fees. Has a five-year time-scale and low-risk tolerance.

She would look at a mix of low-risk funds from a range of different fund management houses. The portfolio might include a unit trust FoF, an investment trust of investment trusts, and UK or international general funds. She might also consider international bond funds and zero dividend preference share investment trusts. She will probably want to keep an element in cash, and use a cash unit trust to benefit from some of the best interest rates available.

TIME'S HEALING NATURE

It is easy to be disconcerted by stock market invest-ment because the prices tend to fall a lot more quickly than they rise. As a result the bad news makes newspaper, television and radio headlines far more easily than the good news. To a journalist a 10% crash in one day makes a good story, but a succession of much smaller upward moves makes no news at all, except perhaps when prices reach record highs.

The reporting of stock market moves in the mass media feeds a misconception about the danger of equity investment. Unless one looks more closely it is easy to believe that stock market crashes are far more significant than they actually are. Of course equity investment has its risks and of course all in-vestors want to avoid them, but given time the im-pact of down movements is far less damaging than is perhaps commonly thought.

Figure 11.2 shows the movement of the FTSE All Share index in late 1987 and encompasses a period including the Black Monday crash. It is an episode which many remember vividly because it gained widespread news coverage. Memories of shocks like these are very off-putting, especially to novice investors, because it reinforces fear that equity in-vestment is dangerous. However, as Figures 11.3 and 11.4 illustrate, the Black Monday crash is much less scary when it is put in the context of a longer time period, a time period over which it is sensible to invest. Over a five-year period with October 1987 in the middle the effect of the crash is lessened (Fig-ure 11.3) and over 10 years the fall can be seen as little more than a blip (Figure 11.4).

Good fund managers take a long-term view. That profits come to young City dealers with smart ideas who duck in and out of stocks and shares is largely myth. You may hear stories about how a

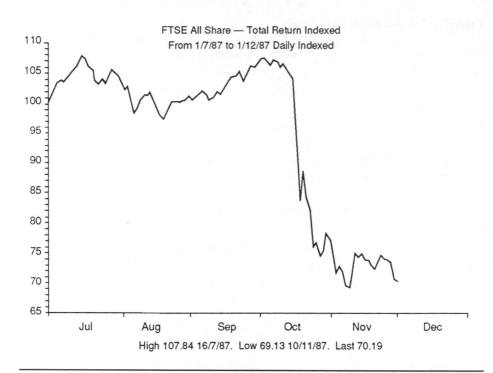

FTSE All Share — Total Return Indexed
From 1/7/87 to 1/12/87 Daily Indexed

High 107.84 16/7/87. Low 69.13 10/11/87. Last 70.19

Figure 11.2 FTSE All Share (July to December 1987). Source: Datastream. Reproduced by permission of Datastream International

particular person made a fortune practically over-night but these again are more the stuff of legend than reality. Most people make money out of the stock market by employing the right mixture of investment judgement and patience.

It is undeniable that the best returns will come to those who avoid the crashes and are only invested when markets are rising. But making these timing judgements is extraordinarily difficult. Even if you correctly predict a market downturn you may sell too early, and then reinvest too late. Jumping in and out of markets may easily leave you worse off than if you stay invested during the bad times.

Richard Wastcoat of investment house Fidelity prepared the following interesting research for me

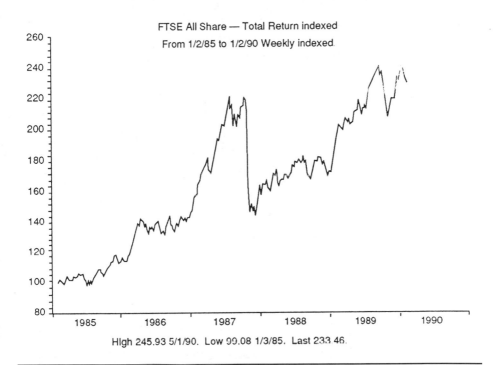

FTSE All Share — Total Return indexed
From 1/2/85 to 1/2/90 Weekly indexed.

High 245.93 5/1/90. Low 99.08 1/3/85. Last 233.46.

Figure 11.3   FTSE All Share (February 1985 to February 1990). Source: Datastream. Reproduced by permission of Datastream International

to reinforce this point. He analysed returns from the UK and US equity markets over the longer term to ascertain the effects on returns of being uninvested on key days. In the study he looked at the period from 1 January 1981 to 29 December 1995 and found that the returns drop dramatically if you miss relatively few of the best days.

If you invested in a fund which reflected the performance of the FTSE All Share index between the two dates the average annualised growth achieved, with income reinvested, would have been 18.8%. But if you missed the 10 best individual days of growth the overall return would have dropped to 15.5%. If you missed the best 20 days 18.8% falls to 13.4% and if you missed the 40 best days during

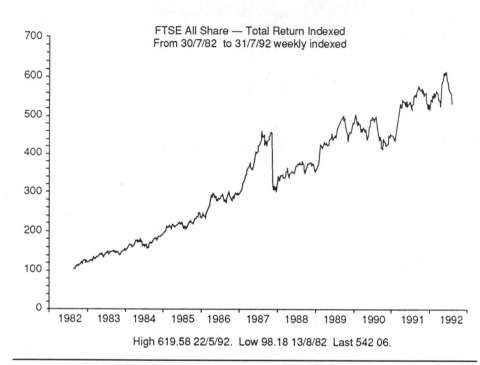

FTSE All Share — Total Return Indexed
From 30/7/82 to 31/7/92 weekly indexed

High 619.58 22/5/92. Low 98.18 13/8/82 Last 542 06.

Figure 11.4 FTSE All Share (July 1982 to July 1992). Source: Datastream. Reproduced by permission of Datastream International

that period—just under 3 days a year—annualised performance nearly halves to 10%. These figures, for the FTSE All Share index and the Standard & Poors' 500, are tabulated in Table 11.2.

Table 11.2 Market timing—the cost of missing the few best days. Source: Fidelity

Market	All days	−10 best	−20 best	−30 best	−40 best
UK	18.76	15.47	13.41	11.65	10.04
USA	15.05	11.94	9.84	8.03	6.37

Index for UK is FTSE All Share Index and for USA S&P 500. Figures are percentage annualised growth rates.

Wastcoat also examined the benefits to accrue from getting market timing exactly right. He looked at the last 25 years of investment, made up three models and measured the annualised growth for each. If you had invested at the worst time in each successive year, that is when the market reached its high point for that year, you would have earned annual growth of 14.7%. If you had invested at the best times, that is when the market hit a low for the year, your performance would be better, but at 17.1% it is not that much better. The third model assumed an arbitrary investment date and Wastcoat used 1 January. If you had invested on each 1 January between 1971 and 1995 you would have achieved growth of 16.3%. He concludes, with great justification, that more money is thrown away trying to avoid stock market falls than will ever be lost by enduring downswings.

Regulation:
The Safeguards against
Sharp Practice

There is a network of authorities which ring-fence investors' money from fraud and offer protection from maladministration and the dissemination of poor financial advice. There is also compensation to be had if things go really wrong. However, you have to invest in authorised investment funds to be eligible for protection. In addition, there is no substitute for sensible investment and keeping a weather-eye out yourself for signs of danger.

SIB, IMRO, SFA AND PIA

In Britain there is a well-developed network of regulators who are responsible for ensuring that individuals and companies who set up unit trusts and investment trust companies act properly.

At the very top is government, which sets the regulatory framework in place through Parliament. Many of the current rules stem from the Financial Services Act of 1986. The Treasury oversees regulation on behalf of the state although it devolves most of the work to the Securities and Investments Board, the senior City watchdog. In turn the SIB gives responsibilities to the other more junior regulators. IMRO, the Investment Management Regulatory Organisation, authorises and monitors investment managers. The SFA, the Securities and Futures Authority, regulates stockbrokers. PIA, the Personal Investment Authority, oversees the marketing side, that is the sales and advice-giving process.

All these bodies have a part to play in the regulation of investment funds. The network of organisations mentioned above authorises all aspects of unit trust investment. However, investment trust companies—as distinct from unit trusts—are also subject to company law and like all companies come under the jurisdiction of the Department of Trade and Industry. Investment trust savings schemes and advice given by advisers who sell investment trusts, however, come in under the SIB umbrella.

TRUSTEES AND BOARDS

In addition to the official regulatory bodies, unit and investment trusts also have supervisors who work internally, ordering the affairs of the unit trust or investment trust company. A unit trust company is called a 'trust' because the assets are held in trust, that is safely, for the investors. Trustees are appointed who are responsible for making sure that the unit trust is run in accordance with the rules set down in its constitution and that it complies with the official regulations established by the government through the SIB. Usually unit trust trustees are professional trustees who will fulfil the role for many unit trusts. A trustee is usually a bank or an insurance company.

An investment trust is not a trust at all, but a company; however, a similar monitoring and safeguarding role to that undertaken by unit trust trustees is conducted by an investment trust company's board of directors. Like directors of all companies, investment trust company directors are compelled to act in the best interests of shareholders, or be liable for disqualification—that is be unable to be a director at any company. They could also be prosecuted.

The assets—that is shares, bonds, property or whatever—are owned by the investors. Decisions about what assets to buy and when to alter the composition of the portfolio are made by the fund managers, who also usually handle the administration. The trustees or board of directors are there to represent the interests of individual investors who are usually so numerous that they need a focal point. In theory private investors could bring pressure to bear on the unit trust trustees or the investment trust's board of directors to press for a change in the way a fund is run, but in practice it is very difficult to get a private investor's voice heard.

Cynics can easily argue with nudges and winks that trustees or boards of directors are little more than the puppets of fund management companies who launch and largely run many of the big funds. Trustees and directors earn a fee and maybe want other similar comfortable appointments from fund manager-administrators; so they are, it could be inferred, unlikely to want to rock the boat. There may be some truth in this innuendo but it is surely more satisfactory to have people in place to check and balance the movements of a fund manager on behalf of investors than have no such coverage.

CRIMES, CONSPIRACIES AND CONFUSIONS

If things do go awry it is at least as likely that you will be on the receiving end of incompetency or maladministration as it is possible you are criminally defrauded. Many of the frauds perpetrated in recent years have been connected with schemes operating outside the UK regulatory regime. If the investment fund, investment fund manager and your financial advisers are all properly regulated it is a good deal more likely that if things go wrong it is down to administrative malaise than wrong doing.

Big investment management firms have reputations to protect and if enough of a fuss is made it is likely they will cough up in order to minimise adverse impact on their reputations. It is not quite the same arena but it may be useful to note here that the damage caused by the collapse of the Maxwell empire—the largest-scale fraud to affect private individuals in recent history—was largely repaired thanks to a series of payments from financial institutions keen to preserve their own reputations and that of the system as a whole. In the collapse of Barings Bank in 1995 it was notable that the assets of the Barings unit trusts were protected from being drawn into the fiasco because the assets in the trust were not owned by Barings but by the unit holders, and held in trust by trustees.

If financial recompense is not offered voluntarily in order to shore up a reputation regulators may force or at least oblige companies to make good the cost of mistakes or fraud.

One way or another, most unfortunately, and despite the existence of a pretty comprehensive network of regulators, crimes, conspiracies and confusions happen. There is no point in trying to pretend that we live in a perfect world or that any watchdog system is foolproof. Fault may always be found. To admit the existence of the dark side is not to excuse it, but the risks of falling victim ought to be kept in perspective. In developed economies like ours the chance that invested money is fraudulently siphoned away is a small one. In addition, it is critical to weigh the risk that you will suffer a loss through investment funds with the dangers inherent in other kinds of investment. History tells us that there is small risk of being defrauded investing in equities but that there is a very large risk—in fact it is almost a certainty—that if you invest in deposits the value of your money measured against inflation will fall.

If the worst does come to the worst and you do lose money and the company or individual cannot pay compensation you may qualify for recompense under the Investors Compensation Scheme. The ICS is an arm of the SIB and is funded by a levy on all investment firms. It pays 100% of any valid claim up to £30,000 and 90% of another £20,000 making a maximum payout of £48,000. Pursuing claims can be a tortuous and long process, however.

It is perhaps worth noting here that in the past the most successful claims have come after consumers have been given negligent financial advice and most of these concern cases where financial products are recommended which are entirely inappropriate to an individual investor's needs.

Remember one last point. You have no grounds for complaint if you simply choose, or have chosen on your behalf, investments which produce disappointing performance. Regulation offers no protection against mistakes of investment judgement.

HOW TO COMPLAIN AND GAIN RECOMPENSE

If you have been defrauded or the subject of an administrative confusion the first place to turn is the company from which you received the bad treatment. After that you should try one of the Ombudsman schemes. Ombudsman schemes are voluntary and decisions made by an adjudication of this sort are not usually legally binding. However, Ombudsmen have a fair amount of moral weight to throw around and companies do abide by most of the decisions made. You can also approach regulators direct but in many instances you are likely to be referred to an Ombudsman.

The relevant Ombudsman offices for investment fund complaints are the PIA Ombudsman, the Investment Ombudsman and possibly the Insurance Ombudsman. The Ombudsman you need will depend on particular circumstances, but one Ombudsman will refer you to another more appropriate one if it cannot help itself. The addresses are in Appendix 3.

INVESTOR BEST PRACTICE

The internal and external control mechanisms are comprehensive. However, it is a foolish investor who takes it for granted that issues of security and propriety are automatically taken care of on his or her behalf. If things do go wrong there is a chance that recompense of some kind will be available. But, and it is a big but, an investment has to be within the framework of regulation for an investor to qualify for redress. That means that at every stage you ought to check that a unit trust, an investment trust, the fund managers, financial advisers and other salespeople are properly authorised. The SIB has a central register of authorised firms and consumers are encouraged to contact it. The telephone number is 0171 929 3652. Investors should not only check that a firm or individual is authorised but also authorised for the kind of business you are putting his or her way. There are various different levels of authorisation, particularly those applicable to financial advisers.

It is important that you understand an investment. Investments and investment strategies should make common sense. If they do not, and assuming you have made some moderate effort to come to terms with a proposal, it may be best to leave it alone. It is never a good idea to abrogate responsibility for investments. As far as possible take on some of the watchdog role yourself. It is your money after all and it is in your best interests to make every effort to check it is being looked after.

In addition, keep accurate records of what you did, and when. These written records should include the timing and content of telephone calls made, and copies of letters written should be kept as well as all documentation you receive. You should also make and keep notes from interviews with advisers or salespeople. (This may sound like a tiresome obligation, but not only will it make life much easier if things go wrong, it also aids the positive side, the process of monitoring the performance of good investments.)

The Investors Compensation Scheme, guided by one of its former officials David Cresswell, recently composed 101 golden rules for investors. They are well worth reading in full and are obtainable from the ICS (address in Appendix 3). A few, however, are worth repeating here.

- Listen to other people's views but make up your own mind about what is right for you
- Take with a pinch of salt other people's 'winning formulae', especially those you hear at the pub or the golf club
- Be wary of 'get rich quick schemes'
- 'Numbers and small print are boring' is no excuse for not taking an active interest in money matters
- Do not be afraid to ask questions. It is your money and you want to know where it is going
- If an investment seems too good to be true, it probably is

- Bear in mind that slick marketing—free gifts and generous hospitality—is ultimately being paid for by investors
- Ostriches, chinchillas, fine wine, tulip bulbs, classic cars, bloodstock, gemstones, doubloons, Angora goats: these are not legally defined as investments so there is no official compensation fund should the worst happen
- No investment is so urgent that you have to hand over money immediately
- Take time to think over any investment proposals. Do not let yourself be pressured into making hasty decisions
- Make sure you understand how the charges (fees and commission) work
- Before you make your investments check whether any penalties apply should you choose to cash them in early
- Remember that a 'guarantee' is only ever as good as the person providing it.

13 CHAPTER

The Literature You Get: Assessing the Information You Receive

Before making an investment, and while you own a unit or investment trust, you should make a close inspection of the dull and confusing array of literature available to you. This chapter explains how to access the vital information contained.

INFORMATION IS INVESTMENT LIFEBLOOD

It is easy to ignore the literature which finds its way, seeming by the lorry load, through the letter box as soon as you start investing in investment funds. But it would be a grave mistake to cast this paperwork aside. Much of it looks either like boring legalese or over-enthusiastic marketing piffle but in among the rubbish there is information. And without information an investor is lost.

It may take some patient digging to get at the all important facts and figures. It may require that you get accustomed to new and alien phraseology because reading some documents can be like wading through treacle. It is almost like learning a foreign language: the process of familiarising yourself with numbers presented in a profit and loss account or a balance sheet profit can feel like coming to terms with ancient Greek. But if it is important to you to achieve financial security the effort will be worth while. It will also help in other areas of life. Once you can wade through investment fund literature and draw benefit, the terms and conditions on a car hire document or credit card agreement become a stroll in the park.

There are other good reasons why you should take note of the investment fund literature. If things go wrong, or things turn out unexpectedly, ignorance is not necessarily grounds for compensation or recompense. It happens all the time: investors buy into a proposal, it goes wrong, they feel cheated and kick up a fuss only to find that all reasonable warnings were given in the small print. In some ways you ought to welcome reams of small print. Full and proper documentation is usually a sign that a scheme has official government regulatory approval. Of course forgeries can be drawn up, but if there is no small print at all it is a fair indication that a scheme is unregulated and therefore at best high risk, at worst fraudulent.

Another reason for reading the small print is that it can make you a better investor, and one who makes better decisions. As you gain expertise it will also mean you will have to rely less and less on financial advice which can be of very variable quality, and which—one way or another—adds cost. If you are an investor who can make independent decisions they will probably be better decisions. Investing through so-called execution-only dealers can also be cheaper. Doing it yourself could save 5% or more of the original amounts invested.

THE DOCUMENTS TO WATCH OUT FOR . . .

Information is available both before you invest and during the period of your involvement with an investment fund. It is probably more important to make a close examination of documentation before you invest, but the stuff you are sent on a regular basis is important too.

Much of the useful information will be about the investment itself but some, particularly that sent to you during the time you start investing, will concern your rights as a consumer. I will split my survey of the paperwork you receive in two. First I shall cover the documentation you get when you start investing, and then I shall look at the other information. Note that it is important to look at the other information before and during the time you invest.

(A) AT THE TIME YOU START INVESTING

Product Particulars

When a fund manager receives your initial request to buy into a fund he is obliged to send you documents that go by the name of product particulars or 'key features'. This information includes a description of the aims and objectives of a trust, whom it is managed by, who the trustees are if it is a unit trust and who the directors are if an investment trust.

PEPs

If you are wrapping your investment fund investment in a tax-saving personal equity plan you will also have to sign an Inland Revenue declaration that you are entitled to the PEP benefits. You also have to give your national insurance number.

Cancellation and Cooling Off

If you buy a unit trust, or subscribe to an investment trust savings scheme, you are given the opportunity to think twice about your decision. This is a requirement set down by regulators as a way of giving consumers a chance to extricate themselves from hard-sell tactics employed by some salespeople. The opportunity to change your mind comes by giving you the chance to cancel your buy order or by way of what is called a 'cooling off period'.

Fund managers have a choice as to whether they give you a cooling off period or cancellation rights. The difference between cancellation and cooling off is significant. If a firm operates under the cancellation mechanism you are given a two-week period of grace. Also, the fund manager will invest the money in the selected fund as soon as he receives it rather than hold on to the money in cash. If you decide to cancel he will disinvest and return the proceeds to you. With cancellation, therefore, you are exposed to movements in the value of the money provisionally pledged, if the value of the investment fund alters. No charges are levied, but if the value of the fund falls in the intervening period you will not get as much back as you originally committed. In addition, while you lose out if the value of the fund falls you do not gain if the fund value rises. If the price goes up you only get back what you started with.

If you are given a cooling off period your money is not invested until the cooling off period expires. If you do change your mind, therefore, you will get back exactly the amount you initially pledged. At seven days a cooling off period is also shorter than a cancellation period.

With both methods the fund management company will write to you telling you that you have the right to change your mind. If you do nothing, it will be presumed that you are happy to stick by your original decision.

THE SYSTEM IS CHANGING

The procedure for presenting information to investors before they become committed is under review. The aim is to make the process simpler, more easily understandable, and at the same time present investors with more comprehensive information.

Perhaps most significant is the plan to oblige the people who sell us unit trusts, unit trust savings schemes and investment trust saving schemes (but not investment trust outright purchases) to provide an illustration of what might happen to the value of an investment assuming set levels of growth and taking charges into account. If introduced this will amount to a positive move because it will add to the pool of information given to investors, and all information is useful. It is also the kind of exercise that a sensible investor ought to have been trying to do for him or herself anyway, so if it is done as a matter of course it makes life easier. However, it is important to see illustrations for what they are. Illustrations are little more than guesses because anticipated growth rates can be no more than guesses. The most worthwhile part of such an illustration is to see the effect of charges, but investors ought to be careful not to view indications of what may happen to an investment as any sort of guarantee of outcome.

The procedures governing the sale of open-ended investment companies, the new variety of investment fund will adhere to the basic principle here described.

If you buy shares in an investment trust company in one go, either directly or through a stockbroker, there is no cooling off or cancellation period.

THE DOCUMENTS TO WATCH OUT FOR . . .

(B) AT THE TIME YOU START INVESTING AND DURING THE TERM OF THE INVESTMENT

The way in which information is presented by different fund management companies varies. Do not expect information from one investment house to be directly comparable with another because you will only be frustrated.

However, watch out for annual and half-yearly (sometimes called interim) reports. In the case of an investment trust company the annual report and accounts are probably the most comprehensive document available for the perusal of investors. It is also a statutory requirement that the annual report and accounts are prepared and sent to investors. Good unit trust management companies will send regular reports, at least annually, perhaps as frequently as quarterly.

Other documents to watch for are prospectuses. These preview in some detail the fund, its objectives, structure and prospects. The manner in which information is presented also provides clues. If documentation is very ostentatious it is perhaps a warning sign. One way or another it is individual investment fund investors who pay for documents, so if literature is presented with over-the-top flamboyance it may be an indication that a fund administrator is being a little too free with your money. On the other hand very plain documentation suggests cash is short. If the administrators feel unable to give documents a bit of life it might mean there is little money being made from investment either. Style and presentation are not reliable indicators, but do help in the development of an all-round picture.

SEVEN KEY BITS OF INFORMATION

Aims and Objectives

The aims and objectives statement of an investment fund is one of the first useful pieces of information you need to get hold of. It might also come under the heading 'Investment Policy' or something similar. It is important because it gives you a concise résumé of what the fund does. The name of the fund should go some way to doing this, but names can be befogging.

Usually the aims and objectives statement is no more than one sentence, or several bullet point items. A statement could be as simple as 'to invest in equities' but is usually a bit more involved. The Kleinwort Benson General Trust, a unit trust, is an example of the straightforward. Its investment objective is: 'To provide capital growth and increasing income through investment in the ordinary shares of leading British companies'. The wording of the Jupiter Income Unit Trust is equally straightforward but gives notice that its aims are a little narrower. Its fund objective reads: 'To invest principally in UK and other stocks to achieve a high and growing income'.

The Kleinwort Benson Pacific Unit Trust's aim clearly demonstrates its field. It is 'To achieve capital growth through selective investment in securities quoted on the stock markets of the Pacific region, principally Hong Kong, Australia, Singapore, Malaysia, Korea, Thailand, Taiwan and the Philippines'. Likewise, although in a different context, is the Friends Provident Stewardship Fund. It is the oldest 'green' UK-based investment fund and states its objective as being: 'To invest in securities of companies which meet a range of ethical criteria'.

The BZW Convertible Investment Trust is one of the more intricate. Its objective is 'to invest in sterling denominated convertible preference shares, loan stocks and Eurobonds of UK companies whose shares are listed on the Stock Exchange'. Another more specialised fund is the Taverners Trust, run by Abtrust. It was launched in spring 1996 with the promise: 'Taverners will be a new investment trust investing in the securities of companies operating in the brewing and licensed retailing industry. The portfolio will include holdings in companies that produce, wholesale or retail alcoholic drinks and other companies whose activities are related to the licensed trade.'

In all these statements of investment objectives there is an element of jargon, and obfuscation. But the useful information lurks very near the surface.

Portfolio Breakdown

It is a good idea to glance at the shares or bonds that comprise the investment fund. Sometimes this will be a comprehensive list, at other times it will be perhaps the 10 largest investments which are listed.

Almost as important as the actual share selections is the size of each individual share or stock selection relative to the size of the investment fund. A typical fund will have about 50–100 shares or stocks in its portfolio, indicating that the average size of holding ought to be 1–2% each. This will— and should—vary but you might ask questions if the variation is wide. If there are 7 selections each taking 10% of the fund's asset base and 43 others accounting for the rest the fund is unbalanced. If one of the big holdings failed or underperformed the impact on the whole fund would be serious.

Equally, keeping large numbers of small holdings is inefficient. There are flat-rate costs associated with making, buying and monitoring each selection. These costs should be offset against investment returns but if holdings are only tiny, the scope for earning investment profits is inhibited. Widely varying holding sizes also runs contrary to one of the essential attractions of investment funds which is to spread risk and reward earning potential. There may be good reasons to have an outsize holding or two if the investment prospects are astounding. It is sensible to keep high-risk investments small, too, so that if things do go wrong the pain is limited. A balance is required.

If you know which companies are included in your fund, particularly if it is a fund made up of British companies, you can also follow their individual progress through press reports in City pages. This can also be a useful way of learning more about the talents of your fund manager and the process will also add to your knowledge of finance and investment.

It may be worth noting at this point that the disturbing incidents surrounding Morgan Grenfell Asset Management and three of its European unit trusts centred on the purchase of unquoted investments. The managers allowed these to rise, and account for about one-third of the total assets of the fund. There is nothing wrong with buying unquoted shares but it does not really suit the unit trust structure where if an investor wants to cash in units underlying assets may have to be sold to fund the redemption instruction. Unquoted companies' shares are not regularly traded which makes this difficult. Valuing unquoted companies' shares is also hard, because there is no active market, and therefore no easily obtainable and verifiable price. An investment trust, where assets do not have to be sold to raise cash for redemptions, is a much more suitable vehicle for investment in unquoted or other assets where there is no liquid market for exchange, because investors buy and sell without the potential knock-on effect on the underlying asset base.

The reason for bringing this subject up here is that the portfolio breakdown in Morgan Grenfell's annual report clearly showed that this unorthodox stance had been taken by the fund manager.

Manager's Reports

Numbers speak louder than words and performance is best assessed by looking at published statistics. However, useful lessons can be learned from the commentary on an investment period which is provided by managers. This commentary, perhaps entitled the manager's report, should explain in words what happened, why it happened and perhaps give some view of what may happen in the future.

Approval by Trustees or Accountants

Annual reports from unit trusts and investment trusts need to be signed by a firm of accountants as a confirmation that they represent an accurate record of a fund's financial position. In the case of a unit trust the trustees also have to give a similar statement of satisfaction. If either are dissatisfied they may 'qualify' the accounts, meaning that they reserve judgement. This is rare, and such qualification statements are usually terse, dry and worded in a way to give investors only the faintest idea of any failings. Check to see the usual approvals are there, however.

Notification of Charges

It is in the official literature that you should find what the managers take out of the fund in fees. Details of charging structures are outlined in Chapter 8.

Regulatory Authorisation

You should also check the paperwork to see that a firm of investment managers is properly regulated. Further details of authorisation are covered in Chapter 12.

General Information

You may also be sent, or be able to get hold of, general information which may help to improve your overall understanding of investment funds and how they can be used to satisfy certain ambitions. Both trade associations acting for the investment fund industry—the Association of Investment Trust Companies and the Association of Unit Trusts and Investment Funds—have fact sheets which are available by contacting them. Individual fund management companies may also have general commentaries.

Making Choices: The Steps to Wise Investment

This chapter is designed as an investment spring-board. There are preparations to be made, considerations to be taken into account, and action to be taken. This chapter stresses the importance of adopting the right attitude towards investment, and the necessity of all-round financial planning. It will reiterate the need to choose investments which suit your appetite for risk. It will look at choosing a fund manager and describe how to monitor and re-evaluate investments as world-wide circumstances and personal needs change. It will discuss the transfer and sale of investments. It includes a segment on obtaining financial advice and the importance of using information sources and experience in order to learn, and keep learning, about investment funds.

STEP ONE: ATTITUDE

You need to approach investment with the right attitude. The components which make up a good investment attitude are varied and a little nebulous. But if you do not hit on the right mix of ingredients you could find investment a deeply frustrating and worrying activity. You need patience to ride stock market ups and downs and faith that the general patterns of the past will be repeated in the future. You need flexibility in expectation because things rarely turn out exactly as foreseen. You need enough optimism to see and take advantage of investment opportunities when they arise and the right amount of cynicism to cut through advertising and marketing for a product and be able to assess investment proposals for their genuine worth.

Understand that you always pay charges, and that you will win some and lose some. If you do you will be better equipped to invest. To build your own portfolio you need heaps of common sense, a willingness to accept the odd failure and an eye for the main chance. You must also accept that finance, business and economics inhabit a constantly changing environment. Also that there is no such thing as an absolute guarantee, that it is impossible to forecast in any but the vaguest terms, and talk of 'unbeatable' returns is fatuous, misleading or worse.

If you expect that every decision to be taken will be the best possible you will wear yourself out. Investment is a percentage game, and the trick is to try and ensure you make good decisions most of the time. If things do not go right occasionally you should not become exasperated and give up on the exercise. Being a purist or a perfectionist is a hindrance. Even the best fund managers make errors of judgement from time to time. The important thing is to keep things in perspective, remember the overall picture and your overall ambitions.

STEP TWO: ALL-ROUND PLANNING

You should be aware that investment funds play only a part in successful financial planning, and you ought to make investment fund judgements in the context of your overall financial position.

Investment funds are not even the first place to turn, in fact they come some way down the list of priorities. If you have large amounts of debt, in particular non-home loan debt at high rates of interest, it is probably best to delay investment in funds until those debts are either paid off or paid down to small amounts. It makes no sense to pay, say, 20 or 25% interest a year on a credit card at the same time as investing money in the hope of earning perhaps 5 or 10% with an investment fund. It is a question of making best use of your financial resources.

If you are earning you should sort out a pension. It is particularly important if you have access to a company-run scheme because the cost of running personal schemes make them unattractive in comparison. However, if there is no accessible company scheme a personal pension is better than none at all. Pension saving brings good tax breaks, and arguably better tax reliefs than PEPs.

If you have a pension savings arrangement already you ought to bear these in mind when deciding where to invest other money. You might think of investment funds, allied to a PEP, as serving to supplement pension savings. Where PEPs may lose out marginally in tax benefits they certainly gain in terms of flexibility of when you can get access to savings and how it can be used. Pension and investment funds savings share the same asset base, that is they are both invested largely in stocks and shares. It makes sense, therefore, to find out where your pension savings are invested so that you can buy investment funds which complement the pension investment. For example, pension savings may be in very stable funds—managed or general funds—and you could think of your investment funds savings as giving the opportunity to run more risk in the hope of earning greater reward.

Investment funds only play a part—albeit an important part—in overall financial planning. A good portfolio will include short-term deposits where you can get easy access to money in case of emergency as well as longer-term equity investments. National Savings products, bond investment—perhaps through investment funds or by buying British government gilts or even special building society fixed-term investments—also have a role to play.

You should not compartmentalise your wealth. All elements—debt, pensions, investment funds, a house, individual company shares—ought to be borne in mind together when you decide where, when and how to invest. For example, if you own a house—or are paying a mortgage on one—it is likely to account for a large part of your overall wealth and will give you significant exposure to property prices. It may not be wise to duplicate exposure to property in the campaign to create a well-balanced financial position. If you have an endowment policy, a long-term stock market saving scheme itself which is linked to your mortgage should come into the equation.

STEP THREE: ASSESS YOUR APPETITE FOR RISK

Prime among the requirements on any investor is to decide how much risk you are prepared to take on. That is not to say that all investments have to fit your overall risk profile. Different investments with different risks attached might be collected together to build a portfolio which satisfies the broader requirement. It is probably best for the vast majority of people to build up a core of safe and reliable investments first, and then branch out.

STEP FOUR: OBTAINING INFORMATION

The easiest way to go about investing in an investment fund is to trawl through the personal finance sections of the national papers and look for adverts from the management companies. You can then cut out the coupons or telephone the special numbers, and wait for relevant information and application forms to be sent to you. The editorial in the personal finance sections may also provide information about investment funds.

In national newspapers the most comprehensive personal finance and investment fund coverage is given by the *Telegraph, Times, Guardian* and *Independent* and *Financial Times* on Saturdays and by the *Sunday Times, Mail on Sunday, Sunday Express, Sunday Telegraph, Observer* and *Independent on Sunday* on, obviously, Sundays. The *Daily Mail* and the *Daily Express* have personal finance sections on Wednesdays.

You can get good information through press advertisements and press editorials but it is restrictive. Not all fund managers will advertise, and they may not advertise those investment funds which would suit you best. Fund managers who are good at marketing may not also be good at long term fund management (although it is just as true to say that poor investment performers shy away from publicity out of embarrassment). Adverts may be for new products too, and in many cases the old tried and tested investment funds are more practically useful. Personal finance press articles may also give exposure to new ideas when old boring ones are more relevant to your particular situation too. Personal finance journalists also write articles to mirror the general news or business news agenda and again, this agenda may not coincide with an individual investor's priorities.

The press may be a slightly haphazard place to glean information, but there is a lot there. Attention should also be paid to wider business and economic issues, even more general items in political, home and foreign pages. The investment arena is not an isolated place but one which lives, breeds and is fearful of real world events. It makes sense, therefore, for an investor to keep abreast of current affairs.

Personal finance coverage addresses general issues as well as passing comment on specific funds. Generic information is also available from the two investment fund trade associations, AITC and AUTIF, which publish fact sheets and investor guides. Individual fund management companies, high street banks and building societies, and firms of independent financial advisers and stockbrokers also produce pamphlets. *Which?*, the magazine of the Consumers' Association, also writes regularly about investment funds and related issues and it may be useful to subscribe, or obtain a back issue which covers the subject.

The importance of information and understanding means a thorough investor will look for and learn from information from many or all of these sources. Investment is often shrouded in jargon and a false halo of mysticism but it is founded in common sense. None the less it is a good idea to arm yourself with a glossary of terms. You can buy books which are nothing else but glossaries of financial lingo, and these can be good for quick cross-reference.

A more systematic and thorough survey of investment funds is possible by immersing yourself in the performance tables of *Money Management*, or one of the other monthly heavyweight magazines such as *Planned Savings* or *Money Observer*. Reading performance tables is only a little more exciting than watching paint dry but it is one of the few ways an individual can make a comprehensive assessment of the important attributes of different funds. Here can be found how a fund has performed, how large it is, how old it is and here is where different sorts of fund can be compared with one another.

Appendices 1 and 2 list contact information for all the main groups which run unit trusts or investment trusts so you can approach a particular manager directly for further information on funds you like the look of.

STEP FIVE: OBTAINING FINANCIAL ADVICE

There is one other source of information which should not be ignored: financial advisers. If you want help selecting investments—either because you fear you do not have the expertise to handle it yourself or because you do not have the time—financial advisers are an obvious port of call.

However, it is important not to rely exclusively on an adviser. If you think you lack knowledge an adviser should help you through the understanding process, not simply take over. The principles of investment, stripped of confusing jargon, are not impossible to master but the trouble is that advisers—like lawyers—are tempted to swaddle advice in such terms as to make it seem impossibly complicated. Good advisers, however, will not want to dominate and will allow you to play an active part in the process. You should not allow bad advisers to steamroller you. If it is the time you lack to adequately survey the range of investments available advisers can provide invaluable help, but key decisions should be taken by you, the individual investor. Using an adviser should be seen in the same way as employing a contractor to build an extension on a house. The contractor may do much of the tedious leg work, you may take his or her opinion on what materials to use and building styles to mimic, but the initial impetus to get work done, and the final decisions about what exact action is taken, should lie with the individual.

Officially regulated advisers fall into two categories. There are those who work exclusively for one investment institution and who are allowed to sell the investment products of that institution alone. These are known as tied agents. There are also independent financial advisers who have the freedom to recommend products from the whole range available. Common sense dictates that the latter group of advisers are in a better position to give advice. However, there are fewer of them and almost by definition independents are usually single-person or small firm operators. Tied advice is better, perhaps, than no advice at all but if you do use tied advice it is wise to seek it from several sources. Most banks, building societies and insurance/ pension companies—which also manage investment funds—have advisers acting as tied agents, but in this context just because an adviser works for a big institution does not mean the advice is the best on offer.

Professional advice is never free. You pay either consultancy fees for the adviser's time or you could allow the adviser to take a commission from the money you have set aside for investment. Advisers have to declare their commission. Most tied agents will be paid at least some of their wages on commission and many independents are remunerated this way too. Paying for advice by commission can be convenient because it means the cost is spread. But commissions eat into what you put aside to save. If you pay a consultancy fee you can be sure more of your money is invested. You can also be more certain that an independent adviser's recommendation is based on the suitability of an investment and not because one investment-providing institution pays better commission than another. Some independent advisers work on a fee basis but will reduce that fee by the amount of commission he or she earns if an investment is made which pays an adviser commission. This type of arrangement is a sensible half-way house.

Shopping around for independent advice is no less important than shopping around for tied advice. Also look for qualifications. Advisers should at least be in possession of the Financial Planning Certificate, or an equivalent qualification. In theory, the more qualifications an adviser has the better the advice he or she will give. But qualifications are not everything. It is just as valuable for you to come to your own conclusions. If you can put an ultra-cynical cap on and in the course of hard questioning the adviser can remain impressive without disintegrating into talking riddles you may have found a good person to deal with.

It is crucial to see an authorised adviser, and the relevant regulator will probably be the Personal Investment Authority. The PIA demands certain competency standards and if advice given is proved to be negligent compensation could be paid. If you use an independent always make cheques for money to be invested out to the institution taking your money for investment. Unless you are buying investment trust shares through a stockbroker you should not have to channel funds through an intermediary.

STEP SIX: CHOOSING A FUND

Choosing a particular investment fund is a three-stage process. First you need to decide what type of fund you want. You need to become acquainted with the difference between funds which invest in bonds as opposed to equities, then perhaps with income growth funds as distinct from capital growth funds. After that you may want to become more specialist still, and find out about investing in smaller companies or emerging markets.

Second, you need to examine which funds perform well in the sector, and are large enough and long enough established to show pedigree. In these first two stages you should have whittled the choice down to between three and six particular funds. Write off for further details from the managers of the funds on this short list and the final decision can be made from there.

You may want the security of a big name. This has merits, particularly if it is backed by a very large bank or other financial institution. The Morgan Grenfell unpleasantness of 1996 was made considerably less fraught because Deutsche Bank—Morgan's German owner—pumped millions of pounds into the situation to stabilise matters. Other distinguishing features between different fund managers are the clarity of the information presented, the level of service you receive either via the post or when you speak to representatives on the telephone. Charges are important, and you should look at how easy and cheap it is to transfer savings between investment funds managed by the same management company.

First-time investors will have to choose one fund, and one fund manager. But just as it is a good idea to spread money about between funds with different risk profiles it is also a good idea to build investment relationships with several fund managers. A rule of thumb might be that as you accumulate wealth no one fund management firm should look after more than 25% of your savings.

STEP SEVEN: MONITORING INVESTMENTS

Investment funds investment should be given plenty of time to mature. You should certainly not expect to invest for less than three years and it is probably best to think in terms of 5 or 10 years. But close monitoring is important and there will be occasions when it is sensible to liquidate or change investments. Decisions concerning changes to investments need to be taken in reference to the circumstances. As was described in Chapter 11, the difficulty of timing investment exactly means that in trying to avoid downturns you may miss out on the most profitable stock market upswings. Dealing fees, entry and exit charges can also make regular switching an expensive—and therefore performance inhibiting—exercise.

The best reason to sell is because you want to spend the money. This is, after all, what wealth is for. If you have made a nice profit the fear of losing out on more profit should not really stop you selling. In general terms, however, the longer you leave an investment the more profit it will attract. As you get older you may also want to shift the risk profile of your portfolio towards more safety and this will mean making sell decisions.

It is much harder, in many ways, to decide what to do if an investment has done badly. For one thing, to backtrack is to admit you were wrong in the first place. But the world of investment is no place for pride. There is a difference, however, between encountering a rough period of stock market performance—which is part and parcel of using investment funds and probably needs to be endured—and finding yourself on the receiving end of problems which may be more specific to a particular fund.

As a very general rule I would be inclined to sell and take a loss as soon as any fraud (which has a direct effect on a fund) is found, although it is worth remembering that fraud is so rare that it is an emergency strategy most will never encounter. If a particular fund had underperformed its sector average consistently for three years or more—and there was no sign of change in personnel or investment approach at the fund management company—I would also be inclined to give it up as a dead loss. Note that the benchmark I choose is the average sector performance not the top performer. It is not a good idea to be too demanding because high returns may also indicate that a manager is taking greater risks. Not being too greedy is a critical attribute in the adoption of the right investment attitude.

Always remember that a sell decision is only half the decision. You also need to know what you will do with money from a liquidated investment. If you are getting out in good times to spend money that second part of the decision is not hard to take. But if it is poor investment think first where you would get better, or at least more promising, returns.

STEP EIGHT: KEEP LEARNING

You need to adopt a flexible attitude when trying to learn about investment. Do not say to yourself 'I will only invest when I know everything' because that means you will never invest. Do not throw up your hands at the first word, concept or assumption you do not understand because that way you will never get off first base. Instead, make a mental note, gloss over, and the next time you come across a similar expression hope the context makes it more understandable.

There is no substitute for experience. Learn from mistakes and triumphs should come more easily.

Appendix 1: Names and Contacts for Members of the Association of Investment Trust Companies (AITC)

3I,
3i Asset Management,
91 Waterloo Road,
London SE1 8XP.
Tel: 0171 928 3131

Aberforth,
Aberforth Partners,
14 Melville Street,
Edinburgh EH3 7NS.
Tel: 0131 220 0733

Abtrust,
Abtrust Fund Managers,
99 Charterhouse Street,
London EC1M 6AB.
Tel: 0171 490 4466

AIB Investment Managers (UK),
Bankcentre—Britain,
Belmont Road,
Uxbridge,
Middlesex UB8 1SA.
Tel: 01895 259783

Albany Investment Trust,
Port of Liverpool Building,
Pier Head,
Liverpool, L3 1NW.
Tel: 0151 236 8674

Alliance Trust PLC,
Meadow House,
Reform Street,
Dundee DD1 1TJ.
Tel: 01382 201900

**Asset Management Investment
Company PLC,**
6th Floor, Burne House,
88 High Holborn,
London WC1V 6LS.
Tel: 0171 831 0066

**AXA Equity & Law Investment
Fund Managers,**
c/o Henderson Secretarial Services,
3 Finsbury Avenue,
London EC2M 2PA.
Tel: 0171 638 5757

Baillie Gifford & Co,
1 Rutland Court,
Edinburgh EH3 8EY.
Tel: 0131 222 4244

**Baring International Investment
Management,**
155 Bishopsgate,
London EC2M 3XY.
Tel: 0171 628 6000

Baring Investment Management,
155 Bishopsgate,
London EC2M 3XY.
Tel: 0171 628 6000

**Baring Private Investment
Management,**
155 Bishopsgate,
London EC2M 3XY.
Tel: 0171 628 6000

Beta Funds,
3 Bolt Court,
Fleet Street,
London EC4A 3DQ.
Tel: 0171 353 2066

**Broadgate Investment Management
Limited,**
4 Broadgate,
London EC2M 7LE.
Tel: 0171 374 1942

Broker Financial Services,
Whitelodge Farm,
Goose Rye Road,
Worplesden,
Surrey GU3 3RQ.
Tel: 01483 237773

Brown Shipley,
c/o Carey Langlois & Co,
PO Box 98,
7 New Street,
St Peter Port,
Guernsey.
Tel: 01481 727272

**BZW Investment Management
Limited,**
c/o Ivory & Sime PLC,
1 Charlotte Square,
Edinburgh EH2 4DZ.
Tel: 0131 225 1357

Candover Investments,
20 Old Bailey,
London EC4M 7LN.
Tel: 0171 489 9848

Cazenove Fund Management,
12 Tokenhouse Yard,
London EC2R 7AN.
Tel: 0171 588 2828

**City of London Investment
Management Co,**
10 Eastcheap,
London EC3M 1AJ.
Tel: 0171 374 0191

**Commercial Union Investment
Management,**
St Helen's, 1 Undershaft,
London EC3P 3DQ.
Tel: 0171 662 6000

Crosby Asset Management Limited,
25th Floor, No 3 Lockhart Road,
Wanchai,
Hong Kong.
Tel: 00 852 821 3328

CW Asset Management,
12th Floor, Moor House,
119 London Wall,
London EC2Y 5ET.
Tel: 0171 256 8388

Discretionary Unit Fund Managers,
40 Clifton Street,
London EC2A 4AY.
Tel: 0171 377 8819

Dunedin Fund Managers,
25 Ravelston Terrace,
Edinburgh EH4 3EX.
Tel: 0131 315 2500

Edinburgh Fund Managers,
Donaldson House,
97 Haymarket Terrace,
Edinburgh EH12 5HD.
Tel: 0131 313 1000

Electra Fleming,
65 Kingsway,
London WC2B 6QT.
Tel: 0171 831 6464

Ermgassen & Co,
c/o Henderson Secretarial Services,
3 Finsbury Avenue,
London EC2M 2PA.
Tel: 0171 638 5757

Exeter Asset Management,
23 Cathedral Yard,
Exeter EX1 1HB.
Tel: 01392 412122

Fidelity Investments International,
Oakhill House,
130 Tonbridge Road,
Hildenborough,
Kent TN11 9DZ.
Tel: 01732 361144

Finsbury Asset Management,
Alderman's House,
Alderman's Walk,
London EC2M 3XR.
Tel: 0171 623 1363

**Fleming Investment Trust
Management,**
25 Copthall Avenue,
London EC2R 7DR.
Tel: 0171 638 5858

**Foreign & Colonial Emerging
Markets,**
Exchange House, 8th Floor,
Primrose Street,
London EC2A 2NY.
Tel: 0171 454 1415

Foreign & Colonial Management,
Exchange House, 8th Floor,
Primrose Street,
London EC2A 2NY.
Tel: 0171 454 1415

Foreign & Colonial Ventures Ltd,
Exchange House, 8th Floor,
Primrose Street,
London EC2A 2NY.
Tel: 0171 782 9829

**Framlington Investment
Management,**
155 Bishopsgate,
London EC2M 3XJ.
Tel: 0171 374 4100

**Friends Provident Asset
Management,**
c/o Sinclair Henderson Limited,
23 Cathedral Yard,
Exeter EX1 1HB.
Tel: 01392 412122

Gartmore,
Gartmore House,
16–18 Monument Street,
London EC3R 8AJ.
Tel: 0171 623 1212

Genesis Fund Managers,
21 Knightsbridge,
London SW1X 7LY.
Tel: 0171 235 5040

Glasgow Investment Managers,
29 St Vincent Place,
Glasgow G1 2DR.
Tel: 0141 226 4585

Gordon House Asset Management,
5 Half Moon Street,
London W1Y 7RA.
Tel: 0171 409 3185

Govett Phoenix Management,
Wellington House,
Union Street,
St Helier,
Jersey.
Tel: 01534 58847

Graham Investment Managers,
PO Box 641, 1 Seaton Place,
St Helier,
Jersey JE4 8YJ.
Tel: 01534 58847.

Grahams Rintoul & Co,
Cologne House,
13 Haydon Street,
London EC3N 1DB.
Tel: 0171 488 1312

Grofund Investment Managers,
Bankcentre—Britain,
Belmont Road,
Uxbridge,
Middlesex UB8 1SA.
Tel: 01895 72222

Guildhall Investment Management,
Merchants House,
5/7 Southwark Street,
London SE1 1RQ.
Tel: 0171 403 7572

**Guinness Flight Investment Trust
Managers,**
Lighterman's Court,
5 Gainsford Street,
Tower Bridge,
London SE1 2NE.
Tel: 0171 522 2100

**Hambrecht & Quist Asset
Management,**
c/o Ivory & Sime,
1 Charlotte Square,
Edinburgh EH2 4DZ.
Tel: 0131 225 1357

**Henderson Touche Remnant
Investment Trust Management,**
3 Finsbury Avenue,
London EC2M 2PA.
Tel: 0171 638 5757

Ice Management,
9 Devonshire Square,
London EC2M 4YL.
Tel: 0171 929 5269

International Asset Managers,
133 Rose Street Lane South,
Edinburgh EH2 4BB.
Tel: 0131 226 6985

Invesco Asset Management,
11 Devonshire Square,
London EC2M 4YR.
Tel: 0171 626 3434

Invesco Private Portfolio Management,
9 Devonshire Square,
London EC2M 4YL.
Tel: 0171 929 5269

Ivory & Sime,
1 Charlotte Square,
Edinburgh EH2 4DZ.
Tel: 0131 220 4239

Ivory & Sime Asset Management,
14th Floor, 1 Angel Court,
London EC2R 7HR.
Tel: 0171 600 6655

Ivory & Sime Baronsmead,
Clerkenwell House,
67 Clerkenwell Road,
London EC1R 5BH.
Tel: 0171 242 4900

J O Hambro & Partners,
30 Queen Anne's Gate,
London SW1H 9AL.
Tel: 0171 222 2020

J Rothschild Capital Management,
27 St James's Place,
London SW1A 1NR.
Tel: 0171 493 8111

Jardine Fleming Investment Management,
47th Floor, Jardine House,
1 Connaught Place,
Central,
Hong Kong.
Tel: 00 852 2978 7450

John Govett & Co,
Shackleton House,
4 Battle Bridge Lane,
London SE1 2HR.
Tel: 0171 378 7979

John Govett Management (Jersey),
Minden House,
6 Minden Place,
St Helier,
Jersey JE2 4WQ.
Tel: 01534 38578

Johnson Fry Asset Managers,
20 Regent Street,
London SW1Y 4PZ.
Tel: 0171 839 5688

Jordan/Zalaznick Advisors,
c/o Gartmore Investment Limited,
Gartmore House,
16–18 Monument Street,
London EC3R 8AJ.
Tel: 0171 623 1212

Jupiter Asset Management,
11th Floor, Knightsbridge House,
197 Knightsbridge,
London SW7 1RB.
Tel: 0171 412 0703

**Kleinwort Benson Development
Capital,**
10 Fenchurch Street,
London EC3M 3LB.
Tel: 0171 956 6600

**Kleinwort Benson Investment
Management,**
10 Fenchurch Street,
London EC3M 3LB.
Tel: 0171 956 6151

The Law Debenture Corporation,
Princes House,
95 Gresham Street,
London EC2V 7LY.
Tel: 0171 606 5451

Lazard Brothers Asset Management,
21 Moorfields,
London EC2P 2HT.
Tel: 0171 588 2721

Lazard Freres Asset Management,
30 Rockefeller Plaza,
New York,
NY 10020, USA.
Tel: 001 212 632 6000

**Legal & General Investment
Management,**
Bucklersbury House,
3 Queen Victoria Street,
London EC4N 8EL.
Tel: 0171 528 6883

Legal & General Ventures Limited,
9th Floor, Temple Court,
11 Queen Victoria Street,
London EC4N 4TP.
Tel: 0171 489 1888

**Liechtenstein Global Trust Asset
Management,**
8 Devonshire Square (8th Floor),
London EC2M 4YJ.
Tel: 0171 710 4567

**Lloyd George Investment
Management,**
c/o Raphael Zorn Hemsley,
10 Throgmorton Avenue,
London EC2N 2DP.
Tel: 0171 628 4000

Lloyds Investment Managers,
48 Chiswell Street,
London EC1Y 4GR.
Tel: 0171 600 4500

Majedie Investments,
1 Minster Court,
Mincing Lane,
London EC3R 7ZZ.
Tel: 0171 626 1243

**Management International
(Guernsey),**
Bermuda House,
St Julian's Avenue,
St Peter Port,
Guernsey,
Channel Islands GY1 3NF.
Tel: 01481 726268

Marathon Asset Management,
Dragon Court,
27–29 Macklin Street,
London WC2B 5LX.
Tel: 0171 404 6364

**Martin Currie Investment
Management,**
Saltire Court,
20 Castle Terrace,
Edinburgh EH1 2ES.
Tel: 0131 229 5252

Maxwell Meighen & Associates,
110 Yonge Street,
Suite 1601,
Toronto,
Ontario,
Canada M5C 1T4.
Tel: 001 416 366 2931

Mercury Asset Management,
33 King William Street,
London EC4R 9AS.
Tel: 0171 280 2800

Montanaro Investment Managers,
c/o Sinclair Henderson Limited,
23 Cathedral Yard,
Exeter EX1 1HB.
Tel: 01392 412122

Moorgate Investment Management,
49 Hay's Mews,
London W1X 8NS.
Tel: 0171 409 3419

Morgan Grenfell Trust Managers,
20 Finsbury Circus,
London EC2M 1NB.
Tel: 0171 256 7500

Murray Johnstone,
7 West Nile Street,
Glasgow G1 2PX.
Tel: 0141 226 3131

Natwest Investment Management,
Fenchurch Exchange,
8 Fenchurch Place,
London EC3M 4TE.
Tel: 0171 374 3000

NM Funds Management (Europe),
1 Chaseside,
Bournemouth BH7 7DD.
Tel: 01202 303130

Northern Venture Managers,
Northumberland House,
Princess Square,
Newcastle upon Tyne NE1 8ER.
Tel: 0191 232 7068

**Old Mutual International Asset
Managers (Guernsey),**
Fairbairn House,
Rohais,
St Peter Port,
Guernsey,
Channel Islands.
Tel: 01481 726726.

Old Mutual Portfolio Managers,
Providence House,
2 Bartley Way,
Hook,
Basingstoke,
Hants RG27 9XA.
Tel: 01256 743361

Olim,
Pollen House,
10–12 Cork Street,
London W1X 1PD.
Tel: 0171 439 4400.

Pantheon Ventures,
43–44 Albemarle Street,
Mayfair,
London W1X 3FE.
Tel: 0171 493 5685

Paribas Asset Management Limited,
2–3 Philpot Lane,
London EC3M 8AQ.
Tel: 0171 621 1161

Perpetual Portfolio Management,
48 Hart Street,
Henley-on-Thames,
Oxon RG9 2AZ.
Tel: 01491 417280

Personal Assets Trust,
1 Charlotte Square,
Edinburgh EH2 4DZ.
Tel: 0131 225 1357

Pictet Asset Management UK,
Cutlers Gardens,
5 Devonshire Square,
London EC2M 4LD.
Tel: 0171 972 6800

Prolific Asset Management,
Walbrook House,
23 Walbrook,
London EC4N 8LD.
Tel: 0171 280 3700

**REA Brothers (Investment
Management),**
Alderman's House,
Alderman's Walk,
London EC2M 3XR.
Tel: 0171 623 1155

River & Mercantile Investment Management,
7 Lincoln's Inn Fields,
London WC2A 3BP.
Tel: 0171 405 7722

Robert Fleming Management (Jersey),
c/o Fleming Investment Management,
25 Copthall Avenue,
London EC2R 7DR.
Tel: 0171 638 5858

Rothschild Asset Management Limited,
Five Arrows House,
St Swithin's Lane,
London EC4N 8NR.
Tel: 0171 623 1000

Rutherford Asset Management Limited,
99 Charterhouse Street,
London EC1M 6HR.
Tel: 0171 490 3882

Schroder Investment Management,
Senator House,
85 Queen Victoria Street,
London EC4V 4EJ.
Tel: 0171 382 6000

Scottish Amicable Investment Managers,
The Grosvenor Building,
72 Gordon Street,
Glasgow G1 3RS.
Tel: 0141 248 2323

Scottish Investment Trust,
6 Albyn Place,
Edinburgh EH2 4NL.
Tel: 0131 225 7781

Scottish Value Management,
2 Canning Street Lane,
Edinburgh EH3 8ER.
Tel: 0131 229 1100

Scudder, Stevens & Clark,
New London House,
6 London Street,
London EC3R 7BE.
Tel: 0171 264 5000

Second Alliance Trust,
Meadow House,
Reform Street,
Dundee DD1 1TJ.
Tel: 01382 201900

SFM Investment Management Limited,
16 Newton Place,
Glasgow G3 7PY.
Tel: 0141 332 2334

Sloane Robinson Investment Management,
Den Norske (Bank Building),
20 St Dunstan's Hill,
London EC3R 8HY.
Tel: 0171 929 2771

Stewart Ivory & Co,
45 Charlotte Square,
Edinburgh EH2 4HW.
Tel: 0131 226 3271

Sun Life Investment Management Services,
107 Cheapside,
London EC2V 6DU.
Tel: 0171 606 7788

Templeton Investment Management,
Saltire Court,
20 Castle Terrace,
Edinburgh EH1 2EH.
Tel: 0131 469 4000

Thornton Investment Management,
Swan House,
33 Queen Street,
London EC4R 1AX.
Tel: 0171 246 3000

Trust of Property Shares,
Fifth Floor,
77 South Audley Street,
London W1Y 6EE.
Tel: 0171 486 4684

Venturi Investment Management,
Burne House,
88 High Holborn,
London WC1V 6LS.
Tel: 0171 831 8883

Voyageur International Asset Managers,
133 Rose Street Lane South,
Edinburgh EH2 4BB.
Tel: 0131 226 6985

Wellington Management International,
c/o Aberforth Partners,
14 Melville Street,
Edinburgh EH3 7NS.
Tel: 0131 220 0733

Appendix 2: Names and Contacts for Members of the Association of Unit Trusts and Investment Funds (AUTIF)

Abbey Unit Trust Managers,
100 Holdenhurst Road,
Bournemouth BH8 8AL.
Tel: 01202 292373 Fax: 01202 296816

Abtrust Unit Trust Managers,
10 Queen's Terrace,
Aberdeen AB9 1QJ.
Tel: 01224 631999 Fax: 01224 633102

AIB Unit Trust Managers,
Young James House,
51 Belmont Road,
Uxbridge,
Middlesex UB8 1RZ.
Tel: 01895 259783 Fax: 01895 810554

Airways Unit Trust Managers,
1 Douglas Road,
Stanwell,
Staines,
Middlesex TW19 7QS.
Tel: 01784 247311 Fax: 01784 242944

Albert E Sharp Fund Managers,
Temple Cowe,
35 Bull Street,
Birmingham B4 6ES.
Tel: 0121 200 2244 Fax: 0121 212 0779

Allchurches Investment Management Services,
Beaufort House,
Brunswick Road,
Gloucester GL1 1JZ.
Tel: 01452 305958 Fax: 01452 311690

Allied Dunbar Unit Trusts,
Allied Dunbar Centre,
Station Road,
Swindon,
Wiltshire SN1 1EL.
Tel: 01793 514514 Fax: 01793 503491

**AXA Equity & Law Unit Trust
Managers Ltd,**
AXA Equity & Law House,
Corporation Street,
Coventry CV1 1GD.
Tel: 01203 553231 Fax: 01203 227734

Baillie Gifford & Co,
1 Rutland Court,
Edinburgh EH3 8EY.
Tel: 0131 222 4244 Fax: 0131 222 4490

**B & CE Unit Trust Management
Company,**
Manor Royal,
Crawley,
West Sussex RH10 2QP.
Tel: 01293 526911 Fax: 01293 526933

Bank of Ireland Fund Managers,
36 Queen Street,
London EC4R 1BN.
Tel: 0171 489 8673 Fax: 0171 489 9676

Barclays Unicorn,
Fleetway House,
25 Farringdon Street,
London EC4A 4JA.
Tel: 0800 374 373 Fax: 0171 832 3944

Baring Fund Managers,
155 Bishopsgate,
London EC2M 3XY.
Tel: 0171 628 6000 Fax: 0171 638 7928

Britannia Fund Managers,
50 Bothwell Street,
Glasgow G2 6HR.
Tel: 0141 248 2000 Fax: 0141 223 6000

Burrage Unit Trust Management,
117 Fenchurch Street,
London EC3M 5AL.
Tel: 0171 480 7216 Fax: 0171 488 1848

**BWD Rensburg Unit Trust
Managers,**
Woodsome House,
Woodsome Park,
Fenay Bridge,
Huddersfield,
West Yorkshire HD8 0JG.
Tel: 01484 602250 Fax: 01484 604099

Canada Life Management (UK),
Canada Life Place,
High Street,
Potters Bar,
Hertfordshire EN6 5BA.
Tel: 01707 651122 Fax: 01707 646088

**Capel Cure Myers Unit Trust
Management,**
The Registry,
Royal Mint Court,
London EC3N 4EY.
Tel: 0171 488 4000 Fax: 0171 480 5695

Cazenove Unit Trust Management,
3 Copthall Avenue,
London EC2R 7BH.
Tel: 0171 606 0708 Fax: 0171 606 9205

CIS Unit Managers,
CIS Buildings,
Miller Street,
Manchester M60 0AL.
Tel: 0161 837 5060 Fax: 0161 837 5070

City Financial Unit Trust Managers,
1 White Hart Yard,
London Bridge,
London SE1 1NX.
Tel: 0171 407 5966 Fax: 0171 407 5265

City of London Unit Trust Managers,
10 Eastcheap,
London EC3M 1AJ.
Tel: 0171 374 0191 Fax: 0171 374 2063

Clerical Medical Unit Trust Managers,
Narrow Plain,
Bristol BS2 0JH.
Tel: 0800 373369 Fax: 01275 554031

Colonial Mutual Unit Trust Managers Ltd,
Colonial Mutual House,
Quayside,
Chatham Maritime,
Kent ME4 4YY.
Tel: 01634 890000 Fax: 01634 898985

Commercial Union Fin Man International,
Exchange Court,
3 Bedford Park,
Croydon CR9 2ZL.
Tel: 0181 686 9818 Fax: 0171 662 5850

Consistent Unit Trust Management Company,
111 Cannon Street,
London EC4N 5AR.
Tel: 0171 283 0114 Fax: 0171 283 0979

Credit Suisse Investment Funds (UK),
Beaufort House,
15 St Botolph Street,
London EC3A 7JJ.
Tel: 0171 426 2929 Fax: 0171 426 2959

Discretionary Unit Fund Managers,
40 Clifton Street,
London EC2A 4AY.
Tel: 0171 377 8819 Fax: 0171 377 0353

Dunedin Unit Trust Managers,
Dunedin House,
25 Ravelston Terrace,
Edinburgh EH4 3EX.
Tel: 0131 315 2500 Fax: 0131 315 2222

Eagle Star Unit Managers,
Eagle Star Centre,
Montpellier Drive,
Cheltenham,
Gloucester GL53 7LQ.
Tel: 01242 577555 Fax: 01242 221554

Edinburgh Unit Trust Managers,
Donaldson House,
97 Haymarket Terrace,
Edinburgh EH12 5HD.
Tel: 0131 313 1000 Fax: 0131 313 6300

Ely Place Unit Trust Managers,
28 Ely Place,
London EC1N 6RL.
Tel: 0171 242 0242 Fax: 0171 405 4786

Equitable Unit Trust Managers,
Walton Street,
Aylesbury,
Buckinghamshire HP21 7QW.
Tel: 01296 431480 Fax: 01296 39339

Evermore Investment Managers,
1 White Hart Yard,
London Bridge,
London SE1 1NX.
Tel: 0171 407 5966 Fax: 0171 407 5265

Exeter Fund Managers,
23 Cathedral Yard,
Exeter EX1 1HB.
Tel: 01392 412144 Fax: 01392 412133

Family Investment Management,
16 West Street,
Brighton,
East Sussex BN1 2RE.
Tel: 01273 724570 Fax: 01273 207076

Fidelity Investment Services,
Oakhill House,
130 Tonbridge Road,
Hildenborough,
Tonbridge,
Kent TN11 9DZ.
Tel: 0800 414161 Fax: 01732 838886

Fleming Private Fund Management Ltd,
20 Finsbury Street,
London EC2Y 9AQ.
Tel: 0171 814 2762 Fax: 0171 814 2800

Foreign & Colonial Unit Managers Ltd,
8th Floor,
Exchange House,
Primrose Street,
London EC2A 2NY.
Tel: 0171 628 8000 Fax: 0171 628 8188

Foster & Braithwaite Fund Management,
3 London Wall Buildings,
London EC2M 5RB.
Tel: 0171 588 6111 Fax: 0171 256 5505

Framlington Unit Management,
155 Bishopsgate,
London EC2M 3FT.
Tel: 0171 374 4100 Fax: 0171 330 6644

Friends Provident Unit Trust Managers,
Enterprise House,
Isambard Brunel Road,
Portsmouth,
Hampshire PO1 2AW.
Tel: 01705 881340 Fax: 01705 881320

GA Unit Trust Managers,
2 Rougier Street,
York YO1 1HR.
Tel: 01904 628982 Fax: 01904 611411

Gan Unit Trust Management,
Gan House,
Harlow,
Essex CM20 2EW.
Tel: 01279 626262 Fax: 01279 626133

Gartmore Fund Managers,
Gartmore House,
16–18 Monument Street,
London EC3R 8AJ.
Tel: 0800 289336 Fax: 0171 782 2075

GEM Dolphin Investment Managers,
5 Giltspur Street,
London EC1A 9BD.
Tel: 0171 236 6441 Fax: 0171 236 0121

Granville Unit Trust Management,
Mint House,
77 Mansell Street,
London E1 8AF.
Tel: 0171 488 1212 Fax: 0171 481 3911

GT Global Fund Management,
Alban Gate,
14th Floor,
125 London Wall,
London EC2Y 5AS.
Tel: 0171 710 4567 Fax: 0171 696 0966

Guinness Flight Unit Trust Managers,
Lighterman's Court,
5 Gainsford Street,
London SE1 2NE.
Tel: 0171 522 2109 Fax: 0171 522 2102

Halifax Unit Trust Management,
Trinity Road,
Halifax,
West Yorkshire HX1 2RG.
Tel: 0171 220 5050 Fax: 0171 220 5056

Hambros Unit Trust Managers,
41 Tower Hill,
London EC3N 4HA.
Tel: 0800 289895 Fax: 0171 702 4424

Hansard Unit Trust Managers,
Liberty House,
Station Road,
New Barnet,
Hertfordshire EN5 1PA.
Tel: 0181 440 8210 Fax: 0181 441 2208

Henderson Touche Remnant Unit Trust Management,
3 Finsbury Avenue,
London EC2M 2PA.
Tel: 0171 638 5757 Fax: 0171 377 5742

Henry Cooke Investment Funds,
1 King Street,
Manchester M2 6AW.
Tel: 0800 526358 Fax: 0161 832 9051

Hill Samuel Unit Trust Managers,
10 Fleet Place,
London EC4M 7RH.
Tel: 0171 203 3000 Fax: 0171 203 3030

HSBC Unit Trust Management,
6 Bevis Marks,
London EC3A 7QP.
Tel: 0171 955 5050 Fax: 0171 955 5052

Invesco Fund Managers Ltd,
11 Devonshire Square,
London EC2M 4YR.
Tel: 0800 010 733 Fax: 0171 623 3339

John Govett Unit Trust Management,
Shackleton House,
4 Battle Bridge Lane,
London SE1 2HR.
Tel: 0171 378 7979 Fax: 0171 638 3468

Jupiter Unit Trust Managers,
Knightsbridge House,
197 Knightsbridge,
London SW7 1RB.
Tel: 0171 581 3020 Fax: 0171 416 7719

Kleinwort Benson Unit Trusts,
10 Fenchurch Street,
London EC3M 3LB.
Tel: 0171 956 6600 Fax: 0171 956 5810

L & C Unit Trust Management,
2nd Floor, Broadwalk House,
5 Appold Street,
London EC2A 2DA.
Tel: 0171 588 2800 Fax: 0171 374 0066

Laurence Keen Unit Trust Management,
49–51 Bow Lane,
London EC4M 9LX.
Tel: 0171 407 5966 Fax: 0171 407 5265

Laurentian Unit Trust Management,
Barnett Way,
Barnwood,
Gloucester GL4 7RZ.
Tel: 01452 371500 Fax: 01452 372700

Lazard Unit Trust Managers,
21 Moorfields,
London EC2P 2HT.
Tel: 0171 588 2721 Fax: 0171 628 2485

Leeds Unit Trusts,
Permanent House,
1 Lovell Park Road,
Leeds LS1 1NS.
Tel: 0113 243 8181 Fax: 0113 235 8585

Lincoln Fund Managers,
Barnett Way,
Barnwood,
Gloucester GL4 7RZ.
Tel: 01452 371500 Fax: 01452 372700

Lloyds Bank Unit Trust Managers,
Mountbatten House,
Chatham,
Kent ME4 4JF.
Tel: 01634 834000 Fax: 01634 834156

M & G Securities,
7th Floor, 3 Minster Court,
Great Tower Street,
London EC3R 7XH.
Tel: 0171 626 4588 Fax: 0171 929 4987

Maldon Unit Trust Managers,
Beaufort House,
15 St Botolph Street,
London EC3A 7EE.
Tel: 0171 247 6555 Fax: 0171 247 5091

Marks & Spencer Unit Trust Management,
Marks & Spencer Financial Services,
Kings Meadow,
Chester Business Park,
Chester CH99 9UT.
Tel: 0800 363432 Fax: 01244 686116

Martin Currie Unit Trusts,
Saltire Court,
20 Castle Terrace,
Edinburgh EH1 2ES.
Tel: 0131 229 5252 Fax: 0131 228 5552

Matheson Unit Trusts,
63 St Mary Axe,
London EC3A 8AA.
Tel: 0171 369 4800 Fax: 0171 369 4888

Mayflower Management Company,
122 Leadenhall Street,
London EC3V 4QH.
Tel: 0171 303 1234 Fax: 0171 303 1212

Mercury Fund Managers,
33 King William Street,
London EC4R 9AS.
Tel: 0171 280 2800 Fax: 0171 280 2820

Metropolitan Unit Trust Managers Ltd,
Metropolitan House,
Darkes Lane,
Potters Bar,
Hertfordshire EN6 1AJ.
Tel: 01707 662233 Fax: 01707 646828

MGM Unit Managers,
MGM House,
Heene Road,
Worthing,
West Sussex BN11 2DY.
Tel: 01903 204631 Fax: 01903 204171

**Midland Unit Trust Management
Ltd,**
Norwich House,
Nelson Gate,
Commercial Road,
Southampton,
Hampshire SO15 1GX.
Tel: 0345 456123 Fax: 01703 723570

**Morgan Grenfell Unit Trust
Managers,**
20 Finsbury Circus,
London EC2M 1UT.
Tel: 0171 588 7171 Fax: 0171 588 7744

**Murray Johnstone Unit Trust
Management,**
7 West Nile Street,
Glasgow G1 2PX.
Tel: 0141 226 3131 Fax: 0141 248 5420

MW Joint Investors,
46 Court Street,
Haddington,
East Lothian EH41 3NP.
Tel: 01620 825 867 Fax: 01620 826 295

N & P Unit Trust Management,
Alberton House,
St Mary's Parsonage,
Manchester M3 2WJ.
Tel: 0161 839 8277 Fax: 0161 839 8775

**National Australia Trust
Management Company,**
PO Box 3004,
Glasgow G81 2NS.
Tel: 0141 951 2501 Fax: 0141 951 2697

**National Provident Investment
Managers,**
48 Gracechurch Street,
London EC3P 3HH.
Tel: 0171 623 4200 Fax: 0171 280 3355

Nationwide Unit Trust Managers,
Kingsbridge Point,
Princes Street,
Swindon,
Wiltshire SN38 8NL.
Tel: 01793 482300 Fax: 01793 482660

Natwest Unit Trust Managers,
PO Box 886,
Trinity Quay,
Avon Street,
Bristol BS99 5LJ.
Tel: 0117 940 4060 Fax: 0117 940 4799

Newton Fund Managers,
71 Queen Victoria Street,
London EC4V 4DR.
Tel: 0500 550 000 Fax: 0171 332033

NFU Mutual Unit Managers,
Tiddington Road,
Stratford-upon-Avon,
Warwickshire CV37 7BJ.
Tel: 01789 204211 Fax: 01789 298992

Northern Rock Unit Trusts,
Bulman House,
Regent Centre,
Gosforth,
Newcastle upon Tyne NE3 3NG.
Tel: 0191 285 2555 Fax: 0191 284 6332

Norwich Union Trust Managers Ltd,
PO Box 124,
Discovery House,
Whiting Road,
Norwich NR4 6EB.
Tel: 01603 683076 Fax: 01603 680677

Old Mutual Managers,
Providence House,
2 Bartley Way,
Hook,
Basingstoke,
Hampshire RG27 9XA.
Tel: 01256 768888 Fax: 01256 768804

Pearl Unit Trusts,
The Pearl Centre,
14 Lynch Wood,
Peterborough PE2 6FY.
Tel: 01733 470470 Fax: 01733 4723

Pembroke Administration,
37–41 Bedford Row,
London WC1R 4JH.
Tel: 0171 813 2244 Fax: 0171 916 1874

Pennine Unit Trust Managers,
Martins Buildings,
4 Water Street,
Liverpool L2 3UF.
Tel: 0151 236 0232 Fax: 0151 236 6497

Perpetual Unit Trust Management,
47–49 Station Road,
Henley-on-Thames,
Oxfordshire RG9 1AF.
Tel: 01491 417000 Fax: 01491 416000

Pilgrim Unit Trust Management,
Commercial Union House,
39 Pilgrim Street,
Newcastle upon Tyne NE1 6RQ.
Tel: 0191 201 3927 Fax: 0191 201 3924

Portfolio Fund Management,
64 London Wall,
London EC2M 5TP.
Tel: 0171 638 0808 Fax: 0171 638 0050

Premium Life Unit Trust Managers,
37–39 Perrymount Road,
Haywards Heath.
West Sussex RH16 3BN.
Tel: 01444 416871 Fax: 01444 452561

Prolific Unit Trust Managers,
Walbrook House,
23 Walbrook,
London EC4N 8LD.
Tel: 0171 280 3700 Fax: 0171 283 9640

Provident Mutual Unit Trust Managers,
PO Box 568,
25–31 Moorgate,
London EC2R 6BA.
Tel: 0171 628 3232 Fax: 0171 374 0145

Refuge Unit Trust Managers,
Refuge House,
Alderley Road,
Wilmslow,
Cheshire SK9 1PF.
Tel: 01625 535959 Fax: 01625 535955

River & Mercantile Investment Funds Ltd,
7 Lincoln's Inn Fields,
London WC2A 3BP.
Tel: 0171 405 3240 Fax: 0171 405 2955

Rothschild Fund Management,
PO Box 528,
Five Arrows House,
St Swithin's Lane,
London EC4N 8NR.
Tel: 0171 623 1000 Fax: 0171 634 2555

Royal Bank of Scotland Unit Trust Management Ltd,
2 Festival Square,
Edinburgh EH3 9SU.
Tel: 0800 716749 Fax: 0131 228 4382

Royal Life Fund Management,
Royal Insurance House,
Peterborough Business Park,
Peterborough PE2 6GG.
Tel: 01733 390000 Fax: 01733 283670

St James's Place Unit Trust Group,
PO Box 26,
150 St Vincent Street,
Glasgow G2 5NS.
Tel: 0141 307 6500 Fax: 0141 248 3778

Sanwa International Investment Services,
City Place House,
PO Box 245,
55 Basinghall Street,
London EC2V 5DJ.
Tel: 0171 330 0572 Fax: 0171 330 0556

Save & Prosper Securities,
Finsbury Dials,
20 Finsbury Street,
London EC2Y 9AY.
Tel: 0171 417 2200 Fax: 0171 417 2361

Schroder Unit Trusts,
Senator House,
85 Queen Victoria Street,
London EC4V 4EJ.
Tel: 0800 526535 Fax: 0171 382 3886

Scottish Amicable Unit Trust Managers Ltd,
Grovenor Building,
2 Gordon Street,
Glasgow G1 3RS.
Tel: 0141 248 2323 Fax: 0141 248 3778

Scottish Equitable Fund Managers,
28 St Andrew Square,
Edinburgh EH2 1YF.
Tel: 0800 454422 Fax: 0131 557 5575

Scottish Life Investment Management Company,
19 St Andrew Square,
Edinburgh EH2 1YE.
Tel: 0131 225 2211 Fax: 0131 225 2586

Scottish Mutual Investment Managers,
Abbey National House,
301 St Vincent Street,
Glasgow G2 5HN.
Tel: 0141 248 6321 Fax: 0141 275 9230

Scottish Widows Fund Management,
15 Dalkeith Road,
Edinburgh EH16 5BU.
Tel: 0131 655 6000 Fax: 0131 662 1301

Semper Eadem Fund Management,
9 Broadlands Court,
Kew Gardens Road,
Kew,
Surrey TW9 3HW.
Tel: 0181 940 7775 Fax: 0181 940 7447

Singer & Friedlander Unit Trust Management,
199 Bishopsgate,
London EC2M 3XP.
Tel: 0171 638 7541 Fax: 0171 762 8487

Skandia Life PEP Managers,
PO Box 365,
Skandia House,
Portland Terrace,
Southampton,
Hampshire SO14 7AS.
Tel: 01703 334411 Fax: 01703 726648

Sovereign Unit Trust Managers,
Tringham House,
Wessex Fields,
Deansleigh Road,
Bournemouth,
Dorset BH7 7DT.
Tel: 01202 435400 Fax: 01202 421988

Standard Life Fund Management,
PO Box 41,
1 Tanfield,
Edinburgh EH3 5RG.
Tel: 0800 393777 Fax: 0131 245 2390

State Street Unit Trust Management,
1 Canada Square,
London E14 5AF.
Tel: 0171 416 2641 Fax: 0171 416 2648

Stewart Ivory Unit Trust Managers,
45 Charlotte Square,
Edinburgh EH2 4HW.
Tel: 0131 226 3271 Fax: 0131 226 5120

Sun Alliance Unit Trust Management,
St Mark's Court,
Chart Way,
Horsham,
West Sussex RH12 1XL.
Tel: 01403 230230 Fax: 01403 234 754

Sun Life of Canada Unit Managers,
Basing View,
Basingstoke,
Hampshire RG21 4DZ.
Tel: 01256 841414 Fax: 01256 57150

TUC Fund Managers,
Congress House,
Great Russell Street,
London WC1B 3LQ.
Tel: 0171 637 7116 Fax: 0171 637 7087

Sun Life Trust Management,
Granite House,
101 Cannon Street,
London EC4N 5AD.
Tel: 0171 606 4044 Fax: 0171 623 8500

United Friendly Unit Trust Managers,
42 Southwark Bridge Road,
London SE1 9HE.
Tel: 0171 800 8000 Fax: 0171 800 8133

Templeton Unit Trust Managers,
Saltire Court,
20 Castle Terrace,
Edinburgh EH1 2EH.
Tel: 0131 469 4000 Fax: 0131 228 4506

Waverley Unit Trust Management,
13 Charlotte Square,
Edinburgh EH2 4DJ.
Tel: 0131 225 1551 Fax: 0131 225 1550

Wesleyan Unit Trust Managers,
Colmore Circus,
Birmingham B4 6AR.
Tel: 0121 200 3003 Fax: 0121 200 9258

Thornton Unit Managers,
Swan House,
33 Queen Street,
London EC4R 1AX.
Tel: 0171 246 3000 Fax: 0171 246 3003

Whittingdale Unit Trust Management,
75 Leadenhall Square,
London EC3V 1LR.
Tel: 0171 623 2444 Fax: 0171 623 2555

Tilney Unit Trust Management,
Royal Liver Building,
Pier Head,
Liverpool L3 1NY.
Tel: 0151 236 6000 Fax: 0151 236 1252

Woolwich Unit Trust Managers,
1 White Oak Square,
Swanley,
Kent BR8 7AG.
Tel: 0181 298 4000 Fax: 0181 298 4885

TSB Unit Trusts,
Charlton House,
Andover,
Hampshire SP10 1RE.
Tel: 01264 345678 Fax: 01264 346800

Appendix 3: Other Contacts

AITC (Association of Investment Trust Companies),
Durrant House,
8–13 Chiswell Street,
London EC1Y 4YY.
Tel: 0171 588 5347

AUTIF (Association of Unit Trusts and Investment Funds),
65 Kingsway,
London WC2B 6TD.
Tel: 0171 831 0898

IMRO (Investment Management Regulatory Organisation),
Lloyds Chambers,
1 Portsoken Street,
London E1 8BT.
Tel: 0171 390 5000

Insurance Ombudsman Bureau,
135 Park Street,
London SE1 9EA.
Tel: 0171 928 7600

Investment Ombudsman,
6 Frederick's Place,
London EC2R 8BI.
Tel: 0171 796 3065

Money Management subscription enquiries,
PO Box 461,
Bromley,
Kent BR2 9WP.
Tel: 0181 402 8485.

PIA (Personal Investment Authority),
7th Floor, 1 Canada Square,
Canary Wharf,
London E14 5AZ.
Tel: 0171 538 8860

PIA Ombudsman,
Centre Point,
103 New Oxford Street,
London WC1A 1QH.
Tel: 0171 240 3838

SIB Central Register.
Tel: 0171 929 3652

SFA (Securities and Futures Authority),
Cottons Centre,
Cottons Lane,
London SE1 2QB.
Tel: 0171 378 9000

Which? Subscription enquiries,
PO Box 44,
Hertford,
Herts SG14 1SH.

Glossary

annualised growth rate total returns over a number of years averaged out to give an annual figure.

bear market negative stock market conditions.

bid offer spread the difference between the price at which an investor buys and the price at which he sells an investment.

blue chip a company or an investment is said to be blue chip if it is has respected and reliable qualities.

bond a tradeable loan certificate issued by a government or a company. British government bonds are also called gilts.

bull market positive stock market conditions.

capital lump sums of money.

collective investment another name for a unit trust or an investment trust. Also called pooled investments, mutual funds and investment funds.

compound growth growth in the value of an investment which benefits from growth in a previous period. Compound growth is, in effect, the calculated growth on growth together with growth on the original value of the asset.

dividend the annual, twice yearly, quarterly or monthly payments made to shareholders as an income on shares they own.

equity is another name for a share. Also sometimes called a security.

execution-only the simple implementation of a transaction request which involves the dissemination of no advice.

gearing the amount of money a company borrows expressed as a percentage of its net assets.

inflation the trend which sees the price of goods and services increase over time. Inflation reduces the buying power of money. In Britain inflation is measured using the retail price index (RPI) from which term comes the expression index-linked, meaning tied to the rate of inflation.

investment trust one of the two leading types of investment fund favoured by private investors. It is distinguished from a unit trust largely because it has a fixed fund of money to use for investment. They are so-called closed end funds.

load an investment or administration management fee.

Personal Equity Plan (PEP) a tax shelter for British and European company shares, equity funds, company bonds and company bond funds.

portfolio a collection of investments.

pound/cost averaging calculation which demonstrates that it can be cheaper to buy unit or investment trusts in a series of regular savings than it is to invest in one lump sum.

return another name for the profits on an investment. Losses are sometimes called negative returns.

tied agent is a financial adviser employed to sell the investment products of one company only. Most investment sales people in high street banks and building societies are tied agents. Independent financial advisers – IFAs – have freedom to recommend all companies products.

total return the most important figure. It is total profits when all levies and charges have been accounted for. May be calculated on an annualised basis.

tracker fund an investment fund which invests mechanically to mirror the composition of an index measure. The performance of a tracker fund will track the performance of the chosen index. Also called index funds.

unit trust one of the two leading types of collective investment favoured by private investors. It is distinguished from an investment trust largely because the money it has to invest depends on investor demand. This is the so-called open ended structure.

warrant an option to buy or not to buy investment trust shares at a specified future date.

weight the part of a portfolio given over to a particular investment or type of investment.

yield the income (perhaps via dividends) expressed as a percentage of the capital value.

Index

Index compiled by Geoffrey Jones